THE
CINEMAS
OF
BRIDPORT

The First Fifty Years

1912–1962

An Outline History
based on *Bridport News* reports

compiled and presented
by
JOHN SURRY

Dedicated to the memory of
SYDNEY CHARLES SHEPHERD
Cinema Manager
1912–1959

First published 1998

Printed by Creeds the Printers
Broadoak, Bridport, Dorset DT6 5NL

Published by J. R. Surry
31a Middle Street, Burton Bradstock, Bridport, Dorset DT6 4QR

ISBN 0-9533544-0-7

Contents

Illustrations between pages 54 and 55.

Preface

The significant role played by Bridport's cinemas in the life of the town – above all in the 1920s and 1930s, during the Second World War and for a decade after it – has received very little attention from local historians, and it is this neglect that the present brief study aims to rectify, in part at least. As will be seen from the following pages, the columns of the Bridport News contain a wealth of relevant material, which is of great social and human interest, revealing as it does the importance of picture- (and theatre-) going to the community and the quiet and beneficial influence manager Sydney Shepherd undoubtedly had on the general well-being of the inhabitants of Bridport and the surrounding area for nearly half a century.

Any history of Bridport's cinemas must concern itself not only (or chiefly) with the buildings and equipment, but also with the films shown on the screen, the live entertainment presented on the stage, the way in which the attractions offered were advertised and the audience reaction to what the management deemed suitable to bring to the town. This account of the two Electric Palaces and the Lyric together with their programmes will, I hope, throw a little light on an important aspect of Bridport life over 50 eventful years of this century, from the opening of the first cinematograph hall in Barrack Street in 1912 to the closure of the Lyric in 1962. I have added a postscript which brings the story up to date in the most cursory fashion. A more detailed survey of these last 35 years or so will entail many more hours of research at the Bridport News offices in East Street.

I am of course principally indebted to all those anonymous Bridport News reporters who recorded local events and whose words are quoted at length. I am most grateful to South West Counties Newspapers, in Taunton, for permission to make extensive use of this outstanding source of information, and to the friendly and tolerant members of the present Bridport News staff (in particular Rosemary Lewis), who have made my frequent visits to East Street most enjoyable – and they only locked me in once. My thanks also to: Pam Herring and Philip Shepherd; the staff of the Bridport Museum, the Dorchester Reference Library and the Dorset County Record Office; the current manager of the Palace, Graham Frampton; Andrew Samways, Bernard Gale, Roger Pinn, John Palmer, Peter Dyson and Frank Crescioli. Finally I would like to thank my wife for photographing the present-day Palace and for tolerating my prolonged immersion in local cinema history, and my daughter Alison, without whose encouragement and editorial expertise this minor contribution to local history would never have appeared in print.

The following publications have been of considerable help in matters of film history and content:

> *Halliwell's Film Guide*
> *Halliwell's Filmgoer's Companion*
> Ephraim Katz, *The Macmillan International Film Encyclopedia*
> BFI Monthly Film Bulletin
> David Quinlan, *British Sound Films – The Studio Years 1928–1959*
> David Shipman, *The Great Movie Stars – The Golden Years*
> *The Story of Cinema Vol. 1*
> Raymond Griffith and Arthur Mayer, *The Movies*
> *Chronicle of the Cinema*
> Patrick Robertson, *The Guinness Book of Film Facts and Feats*

The Oxford Companion to Film
Kevin Brownlow and John Kobal, *Hollywood – The Pioneers*
Clive Hirschhorn,   *The Columbia Story*
                       The Universal Story
                       The Warner Bros Story
                       The Hollywood Musical
John Douglas Eames, *The MGM Story*
                       The Paramount Story
Ronald Bergan,   *The United Artists Story*
Richard B. Jewell with Vernon Harben, *The RKO Story*
Patricia Warren, *British Film Studios – An Illustrated History*

J.R.S.
Burton Bradstock
February 1997

Bridport Electric Palace, Barrack Street

Monday February 26 1912 to Saturday May 29 1926

Bridport News (BN) Fri Feb 9 1912

"As will be seen in our advertisement columns, the Electric Picture Palace will be opened shortly as soon as the hall is completed. The electric installation is now in progress, and the hall, which was formerly the headquarters of the R.F.A. until the new buildings were erected in St Michael's Lane, is being transformed into a thoroughly up-to-date Picturedrome, and an exceptionally attractive programme of animated pictures will be given, with a change twice weekly."

According to the advertisement, which appeared also in the BN Feb 16, the Old Artillery Hall, Bridport (Proprietor: Mr C. L. Shepherd) would reopen as the new BRIDPORT ELECTRIC PALACE.

"Only the Best and Latest ANIMATED PICTURES will be shown. Comedy, Drama, Tragedy, Educational, Trick, Travel, Topical, Comic. The Most Wonderful Sights in the World. Continually changing ...

Open EVERY EVENING 6 to 10.30.

Continuous Performance! No Waiting!

The Public may enter at any time, and the Performance lasts nearly Two Hours.

Popular Prices 3d., 6d., and 1s.

MATINEE on WEDNESDAYS and SATURDAYS at Three O'clock

Admission: Children, 1d. and 2d.; Adults, 3d. and 6d.

D. S. HOLDERNESS, Engineer

SIDNEY SHEPHERD, Manager"

The Dorset Battery of the Royal Field Artillery had moved into its new HQ on Wed Nov 11 1911, the formal opening taking place on Sat Dec 2 1911.

The new proprietor, Mr C. L. Shepherd, also owned cinemas in Arundel, Worthing and Littlehampton. The manager was his son, Sydney Charles Shepherd, who was only 27 when the Electric Palace opened. He was 74 when he finally retired.

Mon Feb 26 1912

The Bridport Electric Palace opened with a programme of six short films: *Circular Fence* (drama), *Maiden of the Piefaced Indians* (comic), *Niagara Falls* (col), *Xmas Carol* (by Dickens), *Night Alarm* (comic) and *Pathé's Gazette*. According to the BN Mar 1 1912 the opening night was well attended.

On Thur Feb 29 the programme changed to: *How Betty Won the School* (comedy), *Josh's Suicide* (comic), *SIEGE OF CALAIS* (col), *Little Moritz Shoots Big Game* (comic), *Pathé's Gazette*.

The staple film fare in these early days consisted of one-reelers, each lasting about 10–15 minutes.

BN Mar 8 1912

The advertisement from now on included the further enticement: CYCLES STORED FREE (at Owner's Risk).

Mon Mar 25 to Wed Mar 27 1912

There was an addition to the programme of six films: "by special request of numerous patrons, the London Coronation Procession." This moderately topical item was shown also in the second half of the week, plus a film of the Naval Review at Spithead.

George V had been crowned on Thursday June 22 1911 and two days later had reviewed 167 British warships and 18 foreign vessels at Spithead.

BN Apr 5 1912

"On Easter Bank Holiday the Palace opens at 11 a.m. to 1 p.m.; from 3 to 5 p.m., and the usual evening programme will be running from 6 p.m. to 10.30 p.m. All pictures are specially selected, and the machine is a perfectly nonflickering one and the eagerness shown by the proprietor, Mr Shepherd, for catering for all classes, makes the Picture Palace thoroughly up-to-date and popular."

On the Whitsun and August Bank Holidays the opening times were similar. In 1913 and 1914 on the Bank Holiday Mondays the afternoon performances were continuous from 2.30 p.m. to 10.30 p.m. – children 1d and 2d to morning performances only.

Mon Apr 22 to Wed Apr 24 1912

Showing of a special film of the Grand National.

Films of major sporting events became a regular feature of the Electric Palace's programmes. These included the Derby, the Boat Race, the Cup Final and important prize fights, but not Test matches. In 1914 the management went to considerable expense to secure the film of the Cup Final played at the Crystal Palace – only four firms were allowed to have their cameras on the ground – and were commended by the BN for their enterprise in obtaining it so soon after the event (BN May 1 1914).

BN Apr 26 1912

"Yesterday (Thursday) the proprietor of the Bridport Electric Palace, Mr Shepherd, devoted the whole amount of takings for the day towards the funds in aid of the Titanic disaster. One more of the hundreds of instances where everyone seems anxious to do something for the sufferers whose friends were lost through the terrible disaster."

The total amount was £9 3s 6d.

The R.M.S. Titanic had sunk on Mon Apr 15 1912, with the loss of 1,523 lives.

BN May 17 1912

"Despite the fact that the lovely weather of the past week has placed indoor entertainments rather at a disadvantage, the cinematograph displays at the Electric Palace continue to receive a large measure of public support. The enterprising manager has secured a splendid film of the great Naval Pageant at Weymouth, which he has been able to obtain for three days only next week, owing to this great topical picture being in such demand."

The film was duly presented (May 20–22) and particularly commended by the BN May 24 1912: "Besides showing the splendid specimens of our first line of defence, it gave a very clear picture of His Majesty and Prince Albert entering their motor cars at Weymouth pier."

They had landed there at 9.45 a.m. on Sat May 11 1912 from the royal yacht, having just spent three days with the Fleet. The King left Weymouth at 10.05 a.m., travelling over the London and South-Western Railway to Walton and arriving at Kempton Park in time to see his horse Dorando win the Sunningdale Park Plate.

Other special films of interesting (inter)national and local events shown at the Electric Palace include:

1913   The State Opening of Parliament; The Tiverton Foxhounds at Wellington
1922   Princess Mary's Wedding and Wedding Presents
1923   The Duke of York's Wedding; The Mount Etna Disaster
1925   New Wembley 1925 – Scenes from the British Empire Exhibition, including the mammoth Circus and the thrills and sensations of the Amusement Park; The Homecoming of the Prince of Wales; The late Queen Alexandra's Funeral.

General interest shorts of a mildly educational type also featured fairly regularly in the programmes, as promised in the initial advertisement. Early examples dealt with such subjects as The Crab and Lobster Industry, Making Birch Brooms, African Sea Birds, Bell Founding, The Flax Industry of New Zealand and Life on the OXO Cattle Farms.

BN May 24 1912 – Empire Day

"By the generosity of His Worship the Mayor and Mayoress (Mr and Mrs J. Suttill) the scholars attending the elementary schools of the town were treated to the Electric Picture Palace, the kindness being greatly appreciated by the children. Barrack Street and the front of the palace were gay with flags in honour of the day, and the troops of children passing to and from the exhibition made it a very busy thoroughfare for the time being."

A photograph of the Church School boys queueing up outside the cinema was taken and issued as a postcard.

The advertised programme for May 24 consisted of *The Last Notch* (drama), *A Zealous Messenger* (comic), *An Excursion to Kabylia* (coloured, travel), *In Time for Press* (drama), *Pathé's Animated Gazette* (topical), *Their First Divorce Case* (comic), *A Flash in the Night* (drama), *Caught with the Goods* (comic). Whether it was all, some or none of these films that were shown to the children remains uncertain. The third and fifth items would seem to be very suitable, the sixth rather less so.

BN Aug 9 1912

"On Bank Holiday a very good series of pictures was given, and in the evening the hall was crowded, many having standing room only, and the patrons consequently suffered through the heat of extra tobacco smoke, while many had a good film partially covered from view by the far too extensive hats, which ladies usually prefer to wear on the occasion of entertainments."

BN Dec 6 1912

"Last week great interest was taken in the local film, which was of a considerable length and gave most of the main streets, and West Bay. This was all the more unique, as it was taken on Saturday, despatched to London, developed and returned to Bridport for the following Monday's exhibition. We hope Mr Shepherd will give another 'local' at some future date, when the opportunity of something of general interest occurs. The film was taken by Mr Holderness, manager of the Littlehampton Palace, which is under the same proprietorship."

Mr Shepherd was to fulfil the BN's hopes.

BN Dec 13 1912

"The hall has been renovated internally, and the screen has been given a coat of white, and other improvements add to the comfort of the patrons, and to the clearness of the pictures."

Mon Dec 23 to Sat Dec 28 1912 – excluding Christmas Day

Included in the programme: a film version of the pantomime Aladdin. In the first few years one or two filmed pantomimes were shown at this time of year.

On Christmas Eve, Boxing Day and Dec 28 the Electric Palace was open continuously from 2.30 to 10.30 p.m.

BN Jan 10 1913

"Each Saturday throughout the English Cup football competition the results will be shown on the screen at the Palace, the arrangements for this being by mutual agreement between the proprietors of the Bridport News and the manager of the Picture Palace."

This information service – much appreciated, no doubt, by football fans in these pre-BBC days – was in operation again for the 1914 Cup competition.

BN Feb 14 1913

"A rumour is whispered in the town that the Picture Palace may be closed, but on enquiry Mr Shepherd assures us that there is not the slightest grounds for such an unfounded report, and in fact Mr Shepherd is making arrangements for a feature film programme on the occasion of the anniversary of the opening of the Palace on Monday February 26th last year, and hopes that the second year will prove as attractive and popular as the first."

The special star picture for Feb 26 only was D. W. Griffith's two-reel re-creation of Custer's Last Stand, *The Massacre*, which returned by request for three days in April (17–19). Patrons were advised to "attend early to avoid the disappointment of finding all the seats filled". The BN Feb 28 reported on the occasion: "Extraordinary scenes were witnessed outside the Palace, the crowd having to be held in check by two policemen. The vestibule was also packed with people waiting for admission, and this continued for about an hour.

We are quite sure that if the manager continues to keep up this high standard of pictures an increased run of prosperity awaits him in the coming year. We sincerely hope this will be the case."

Mon Mar 3 to Wed Mar 5 1913

Included in the programme: a film of *The Bohemian Girl*, Michael Balfe's opera, in three parts – followed a week later by a three-reel version of *Siegfried*, The Famous Opera. The new medium was not afraid to tackle opera, classic novels and plays, whatever the original language, and the young manager of the Electric Palace was not afraid to show these more "serious" works in Bridport. The BN Mar 14 1913 commented favourably on his policy: "The continued popularity of this place of entertainment proves how excellently Mr Sidney C. Shepherd, the manager is catering for the public, and the house is full nightly."

Mon Apr 7 to Wed Apr 9 1913

Along with six other shorts – including *Primitive Potteries of Dorset* (interest) – was *The Green-Eyed Monster*, featuring the great French silent film comedy star Max Linder, acknowledged by Chaplin as his master. The Electric Palace showed several of his 200–300 films, e.g. in July 1912 *Max Linder v. Nick Winter*; in 1914 *Max as a Chiropodist* and *Max and a Daughter of Albion*; in 1923 *Seven Years' Bad Luck*.

Other popular, though now less well-known, early film clowns were Ford Sterling (Keystone cop and comic villain), John Bunny, the Italian slapstick comedian Polidor, and the British comic performer Pimple, who were all to be seen on the screen in Barrack Street in their one-reel comedies. John Bunny was the first funny fat man star of the US studios from 1910 till his death in 1915, while Pimple provided in 1913 and 1914, amongst other items, skits on "Ivanhoe" and Polar exploration.

BN Jun 13 1913

"The chief feature of the programme presented the first three days of this week was a special picture of the sensational race for the Derby. In showing this film so soon after the event the management are to be commended for their enterprise, as towns much larger than Bridport were unable to secure a copy until next week, the films being in such great demand. The picture was taken from six different positions on the course, and clearly depicted the mad act of the militant Suffragette Miss Davison, as well as scenes on the road and course."

At the Derby on Wed Jun 4 Miss Emily Davison had thrown herself in front of the King's horse Anmer, bringing down horse and jockey, and receiving fatal injuries. Her funeral took place on Jun 14.

BN Jul 4 1913

"It might be mentioned that three powerful electric fans have just been installed, which greatly assist in keeping the hall refreshingly cool."

Thu Jul 10 to Sat Jul 12 1913

Included in the programme: "the most wonderful picture ever conceived, entitled 'A BEETLE'S DECEPTION'. The dramatis personae being Real Live BEETLES, DRAGON-FLIES and a DADDY-LONG-LEGS. Must be seen to be believed." This exceptional work was apparently a humorous love story.

BN Jul 25 1913

"Mr Shepherd, the manager, informs us that he has arranged for a film to be taken of the Hospital Carnival tomorrow (Saturday). The exact position of the camera from where the film will be taken will be made known in the morning."

There was a report of the result in the following Friday's BN: "The principal attraction this week is, naturally, the film of the Hospital Carnival, taken on Saturday last. A most excellent picture was obtained of the procession entering South Street from West Street, the tableaux and scenes in West Bay Road being also very clearly depicted, and the successive audiences were not behind in showing their appreciation of the enterprise on the part of the management."

Patrons and others were no doubt delighted, too, when the Hospital Building Fund was given the whole of the proceeds of both matinee and evening performances on Wed Aug 13 1913 of *Theodora*, A Magnificent Ancient Roman Historical Drama ·in

Three Parts, based on a romantic tragedy by French dramatist Victorien Sardou and secured at great expense. "Both as regards acting and scenic mounting the film is one of the finest specimens of photo-play ever seen at the picture palace", commented the BN Aug 15. "In the afternoon the hall was nearly full, and in the evening there was a crowded house to the doors, and the hospital will consequently benefit to the sum of £12 10s. For this occasion, the evening's music was supplied by Mr C. Warren's orchestra, which was greatly appreciated, and again the fine film of the recent carnival was given."

Mon Sep 8 to Wed Sep 19 1913

The programme included a film of *Pickwick Papers* in two parts/reels, with the comic star John Bunny as Mr Pickwick. This was followed in October by *A Tale of Two Cities* in three parts, and in November by *Ivanhoe*, made for £3,500 at Chepstow Castle, one of the first feature films produced in Britain, in six reels.

Other silent versions of classic or well-known novels shown at the Electric Palace include: Ouida's *Moths* (6/14), one of the first US feature films; Daudet's *Sapho* (6/15); *Old St Paul's* (6/16), "an adaptation impressive and accurate in every detail of Harrison Ainsworth's famous novel, and introducing one of the cleverest conflagration scenes (in the burning of old London Bridge) ever presented on the screen"; *The Prisoner of Zenda* (11/16 and 5/19); *Rupert of Hentzau* (11/16 and 5/19); *Silas Marner* (11/17); *The Vicar of Wakefield* (11/17); *Dombey and Son* (11/18), starring Lilian Braithwaite; *The Woman in White* (2/19); *Three Men in a Boat* (12/21); *Kipps* (6/22); *Oliver Twist* (10/23), with Jackie Coogan.

Poetry also attracted the early film-makers – for example, in May 1915 a Most Beautiful Adaption (sic) of Lord Tennyson's Famous Poem – The May Queen appeared in the programme.

Thu Oct 9 to Sat Oct 11 1913

Presentation of a Gigantic Attraction: the Italian eight-reel spectacular epic *Quo Vadis*, described as "the talk of the cinema world" and "the greatest film ever brought into the provinces".

"Special music has been arranged, and an organ installed for the occasion to make a fitting touch corresponding with the old time play." There were also special prices and a children's matinee on Saturday morning at 11 a.m.

With a cast of 5,000 people and 30 lions *Quo Vadis* was an immense success in Europe and America. It had been premiered in Britain at the Royal Albert Hall, where the King and Queen had gone to see it on May 5 1913 – the first British monarch to attend a public cinema performance (in this case a matinee).

The novel was filmed again in 1924, and this Italian-German co-production, with an international cast of 20,000 including Emil Jannings and Lilian Hall-Davis, had a four-day run (Mon Apr 26 to Thu Apr 29 1926) at the Palace just a month before it closed.

MGM's version, made in Rome in 1951, with Peter Ustinov, Robert Taylor and Deborah Kerr, was shown at the Palace in South Street May 6–8 1954, but not, as would have been historically appropriate, at the Lyric.

Mon Nov 17 to Wed Nov 19 1913

The French master criminal Fantômas reaches Bridport in *Fantômas The Man in Black*, the second of five multi-episode films directed by Louis Feuillade. The final three were shown in Jan 1915.

Other series of films, though often less well made than this striking French example, proved to be popular with the Electric Palace's patrons, e.g. the exploits of detective Nick Carter in Paris, and the Broncho Billy films starring G. M. Anderson, who played the cowboy hero nearly 400 times between 1907 and 1914. Two popular British series featured as hero a Royal Navy Lieutenant – Lieut. Rose (Clarendon Film Company, Croydon) and Lieut. Daring (British and Colonial Films, Walthamstow). Between 1912 and 1914 Bridport audiences were treated to at least three of Lieut. Daring's adventures, but the rival Lieut. Rose would seem to have been a less frequent visitor to Barrack Street. In 1922 Aesop's Film Fables appeared regularly in the programme (about 20 were shown), and Felix the Cat arrived in 1924.

Serials, which also helped to make cinema-going a habit, were even more popular, and a considerable number were shown at the Electric Palace, e.g.

1913–14	*What Happened to Mary*, in 12 episodes – the first US serial
1915	*The Million Dollar Mystery*, in 23 episodes, featuring Florence LaBadie
1916	*Greed*, in 19 episodes
1916–17	*Peg o' the Ring*, in 15 episodes, starring Grace Cunard
1918	*Pearl of the Army*, in 15 episodes, a Great Military Mystery Serial concerning the defence of the Panama Canal, starring Pearl White, queen of the silent serials
	Patria, Pathé's Serial Supreme in 15 episodes, featuring the renowned actress Mrs Vernon Castle
1919	*The House of Hate*, in 20 episodes, with Pearl White
1920	*The Lightning Raider*, in 15 episodes, with Pearl White
1920–21	*The Great Gamble*, in 15 episodes
1922	*Miracles of the Jungle*, in 15 episodes
1923	*Elmo King of the Jungle*, in 15 episodes
	Hurricane Hutch, in 15 episodes, starring the thrill-a-minute stunt king, Charles Hutchison
1924	*Plunder*, in 15 episodes, with the peerless serial queen Pearl White
	The Mystery of Dr Fu Manchu, a British serial from the Stoll Film Company
1925	*Ruth of the Range*, in 15 episodes, starring another serial queen Ruth Roland
	Fight and Win, featuring the world's greatest boxer Jack Dempsey
	Into the Net, a New York police serial in 10 episodes
	The Fighting Ranger, in 18 episodes, featuring the World's Champion Stunt Flier Al Wilson and the Popular Serial Star Eileen Sedgwick. Not one idle moment in this Exciting Chapter Play! There's action from the word go – sustained and thrilling to the very last Episode. Chock full of daring, packed with wild riding and hair-raising Aviation Stunts
1926	*Samson of the Circus*, in 15 episodes.

Some documentary features were similarly presented in instalments, e.g.

Over several weeks in 1919: the film of Mr and Mrs Martin E. Johnson's 18,000-mile journey and adventures among the cannibals in the South Pacific

Over six weeks in 1922: the official film of H.R.H. The Prince of Wales' Indian tour (1921–22)

Over five weeks in 1924: *Wembley, the World's Eighth Wonder*, Pathé's great film of the British Empire Exhibition from the commencement to the completion.

It is interesting to note that a revised and condensed version of *The Million Dollar Mystery*, in 6 reels, was shown at the Electric Palace for three days in Mar 1920.

BN Dec 26 1913

"For the comfort of patrons the management have this week introduced rows of very nicely upholstered chairs. The price of these is 1s, and those previously used at this price will be 6d seats, an improvement which will be much appreciated."

Mon Feb 2 to Wed Feb 4 1914

Special attraction: *Gypsy Hate* – "the film that was recently made at West Bay, Eype, Seatown and Lulworth ... features a charming young lady who was successful in winning the International beauty competition, at Folkestone, a few days before the film was taken."

"It was splendidly acted, and some of the scenes, with the cliffs and sea in the background, were particularly fine. On Wednesday evening Mr Warren's orchestra supplied the music, which was a pleasant surprise to the many patrons who attended that performance" (BN Feb 6 1914).

Mon Feb 23 to Sat Feb 28 1914 – Anniversary Week

There were two special attractions:

Mon–Wed *Cleopatra*. The story of a Woman and Queen of Tigerish Ferocity, starring Helen Gardner, who also produced the film. In five parts this was the third feature film to be produced in the US.

Thu–Sat *Hamlet*, starring Sir J. Forbes-Robertson and Miss Gertrude Elliott, supported by the full Drury Lane Theatre Company. Made by the Hepworth Company, the film was one of the first British features. It was revealed in the BN Feb 27 1914 that "attention to detail has been given and no expense spared. For instance, for the ghost scene, at a cost of £400, a castle was erected at Lulworth Cove, and it was only required for three minutes."

"Notwithstanding the great cost incurred by securing these two beautiful productions for Bridport, the management have decided to make no increase in the charges for admission, excepting that 3d extra will be charged for booking to the 6d and 1s seats" (BN Feb 20 1914).

"On two evenings during the week Mr Warren's orchestra was engaged and gave many pleasing selections" (BN Feb 27 1914).

On this second anniversary of the opening of the cinema the BN once again commented favourably on the enterprise: "This place of amusement is now very popular and is well patronized, as Mr S. Shepherd studies his patrons by selecting films that appeal to every class. By so doing he has gained the confidence of the people of

Bridport and the neighbourhood, and we congratulate Mr Shepherd and his staff on the success achieved" (BN Feb 27 1914).

Silent film versions of other Shakespeare plays were shown at the Electric Palace, e.g.

Apr 16–18 1917 *The Merchant of Venice*, with Matheson Lang, Hutin Britton and full London Company – "The Acting and Quality of this Magnificent Production leaves nothing to be desired"

Dec 20–22 1917 *Macbeth*, with Sir Herbert Tree and Constance Collier

Sep 30–Oct 2 1918 *King Lear*, with Frederick Warde, the Great American Shakespearian Actor – "A Remarkably Fine Production, beautifully produced, correct in detail, and a faithful representation of William Shakespeare's Great Play".

A number of more recent theatrical successes were also transferred to the screen and shown in Bridport, in particular the plays of Pinero: *Trelawny of the Wells*, directed by Cecil Hepworth, starring Stewart Rome and Alma Taylor (Oct 1–3 1917); *The Second Mrs Tanqueray*, with Sir George Alexander and Hilda Moore (Nov 5–7 1917); *The Gay Lord Quex*, starring Irene Vanbrugh, England's Leading Actress in her Original and Greatest Part, and Ben Webster. Don't Miss This. (NB, it opened in Bridport on Mon Nov 11 1918.)

Mon Mar 9 to Wed Mar 11 1914

"The customary edition of Pathé's 'Gazette' was also particularly interesting inasmuch as it included a scene of the s.s. 'Dorothea', the boat that went ashore on the Chesil Beach a few weeks ago" – to be precise, on the night of Sat Feb 14 1914.

For some months in 1913 the topical news items had been provided by Williamson's Animated News (mid-May to mid-October), then Gaumont Graphic, but in Feb 1914 Pathé's Gazette was back in place.

BN Mar 27 1914

"The manager, Mr Shepherd, informs us that he has a very costly attraction for his patrons during the present week-end, having secured Pathé's masterpiece 'The King of the Air'. This film, as indicated by its title, deals with the romance of aviation, and it is beautifully coloured throughout and is one of the most expensive films ever shown in Bridport." It contained, apparently, in one scene a very fine example of the tango.

Mon Mar 30 to Wed Apr 1 1914

Showing of *The Battle of Waterloo*, in five reels, with a cast of 2,000, the fourth British feature film to be released in this country. "This film appeals to the patriotism of all British Subjects."

Thu Apr 16 to Sat Apr 18 1914

Included in the programme: *The Wreck* (US 1914), a melodrama about a railroad president involved in a series of feuds with his son and a renegade engine driver. "This should not be missed, and seeing that the railroad smash included in the picture cost the producers £10,000 to produce, is sufficient to say the film is a masterpiece" (BN Apr 17 1914).

The logic of that judgement is questionable.

BN Jul 10 1914

"Despite the summer season, and other counter attractions, the Picture Palace still continues popular, and with the working of electric fans, to cool the hall, a goodly number patronize the pictures each evening."

Tue Aug 4 1914

Britain declares war on Germany.

The main attraction at the Electric Palace during the first half of this week was *True Irish Hearts* – A Grand Production Dealing with the 1798 Rebellion of Ireland. This insurrection by the United Irishmen led to the Act of Union, which came into effect on Jan 1 1801.

The Home Rule problem, temporarily shelved on the outbreak of war, was to come to the fore again with the Easter Rising in Dublin in April 1916.

Thu Aug 20 to Sat Aug 22 1914

Showing of the first of many special films relating to the War. This one included Stirring Scenes in London, Eager to Enlist, Vive la France, Russia, Austrians, The Enemy.

Throughout the war years the Electric Palace showed, in addition to the regular newsreel Pathé's Gazette and one or two major documentary productions, a great many special topical and/or war films. The following selection of titles will give some idea of the varied content:

1914   Our King and Queen with the Troops in Paris; some views of the local battery of the R.F.A. in camp at Weymouth, and farewell scenes at the Railway Station on Saturday last (Sep); A Day with the Belgian Army – This film has only been secured at great cost, and does not contain scenes depicting the horrors of war; The ruins of Termonde – depicting the terrible havoc wrought by the Germans and the pitiable plight to which the Belgians have been reduced; England's Glory: A Special Film of Our Splendid Fleet; Our Lads in Navy Blue (how they are trained); Belgians at Bay; The Fall of Antwerp; Indian Troops' Arrival in France; An animated map of the War

1915   The Bombardment of Scarborough; The King at Ypres; The Battle for Calais; English and French Troops in Flanders; At War with the Turks; The Royal Naval Division – at work and play at the Crystal Palace (By Request of the Naval Authorities); Scenes on the Austro-Servian Frontier; Kitchener inspecting our Allies' troops in France

1916   Lord Kitchener at the Front; The Manufacture of Big Guns – a most interesting Educational Subject; With the Irish at the Front – the first of nine Official War Films presented by Mr Shepherd in response to the request of numerous patrons (Sep); For the Empire – A grand Patriotic Subject, specially arranged, produced and issued by order of H.M. Treasury; The Wonderful Organisation of the R.A.M.C.; Letters from Home; Scenes Around British Headquarteres; Observing for Our Heavy Guns; The King With the Allies, Reviewing Troops, Visiting an Avaiation Camp etc.; Italy's Alpine Campaign

1917   Incidents from the Battle of the Somme (French Official War Film in 2 Parts); Censoring International Mails; Captures on the Somme Front; An Observation Balloon in Flight; Scenes on the Battlefield of Verdun (French Official War

Film); The Franco-British Artillery in the Great Advance; Our Brave Merchant Service

1918 A Special Patriotic Film of Great Interest – The Women's Land Army; Girl Guides at Work; The Surrender of the German Fleet (Dec).

Thu Sep 17 1914

A Grand Benefit Performance, under the patronage of His Worship the Mayor (W.G.F. Cornick, Esq.) in aid of H.R.H. The Prince of Wales's National Relief Fund, of *The British Army. How it is made and used.* "This film, which is in six parts, is the only one taken by the authority of the Army Council ... Mr Warren's orchestra will accompany the film on that evening, for which he has arranged special music" (BN Sept 11 1914).

Thursday's takings amounted to £9 12s 10d and were presented to the Mayor. "The crowded audience was roused to a high pitch of enthusiasm. The management received many congratulations upon securing such an interesting subject ... On Friday afternoon the children from the General Schools and the inmates of the Union witnessed the film at the kind invitation of Mr J. T. Stephens" (BN Sept 25 1914). It was shown also on Friday evening and Saturday.

"The first exhibition of this film was by command of His Majesty the King as a surprise to Queen Alexandra at Sandringham House on the occasion of her birthday in December last" (BN Sept 18 1914). George V's mother celebrated her 69th birthday on Dec 1 1913.

BN Oct 9 1914

"Although it is still impossible to resume the issue of the customary printed programmes, no efforts are being spared by the management to maintain the high character of their pictorial displays."

Mon Oct 12 to Wed Oct 14 1914

One of the films in the programme was the one-reel *Mabel's Strange Predicament*, "which introduced a newcomer to the Keystone Studios in the person of Charles Chaplin, who until quite recently was performing in the Variety Theatres of this country". Mabel was the American comedienne Mabel Normand.

Having toured the US with Fred Karno's Company (1910–11 and 1912–13), Chaplin arrived in Los Angeles in Dec 1913, and in 1914 made 35 films for Mack Sennett's Keystone Studio, *Mabel's Strange Predicament* being the third, released on Feb 9 1914. When he moved to the Essanay Co. at the end of the year, he was described already as the world's greatest comedian.

Mr Shepherd saw to it that his films were seen in Bridport, starting in 1915 with at least 15 of the Keystone films.

Another very popular comic actor, who first appeared as a Keystone cop and in one or two of Chaplin's early one-reelers, was Roscoe "Fatty" Arbuckle, whose films were often in the Electric Palace's programmes from 1914, e.g. *Fatty and the Balloons, Fatty Again, Fatty's Gift, Fatty's Plucky Pup, Fatty's Tintype Tangle*. Scandal destroyed his career in 1921.

BN Dec 25 1914

"At the matinee on Wednesday the usual distribution of oranges to the juvenile patrons took place."

This delightful custom, already established by 1914, continued at the pre-Christmas matinee for some years.

Mon Feb 15 to Wed Feb 17 1915

The programme was to include, as special attraction, a selection of views of the "Formidable" survivors recently landed at Lyme Regis. The battleship H.M.S. Formidable had been torpedoed and sunk in the Channel by a U-Boat at about 2.30 a.m. on the morning of Fri Jan 1 1915. Of her crew of 790, 199 were saved, some of whom – including six dead and three dying – reached Lyme Regis in one of the ship's cutters late at night on New Year's Day.

However, there were logistical problems, as the BN Feb 19 reported: "The programme advertised for the first part of this week went astray in transit, consequently the management were unable to open on Monday evening even after waiting until the eight o'clock train arrived. In order that patrons should not be disappointed the next night, Mr Shepherd telegraphed on Tuesday morning for another set of films so as to be sure of giving a performance that evening, but once more all concerned were doomed to disappointment as the substituted programme shared the fate of the original one and was likewise delayed. However, a good programme was secured in time for the matinee on Wednesday."

Mon Feb 22 to Sat Feb 27 1915 – Third Anniversary Week

The special attractions were:

Mon–Wed *England's Menace*, a London Film company production, depicting the invasion of England by a foreign power.

Thu–Sat The Cunard Company's Magnificent Patriotic Production *The Call of the Drum*. Mr Warren's orchestra supplied the music on the Thursday evening.

"During the past year, despite the seven months of war, the Palace has been well patronised, this being largely due to the enterprise of Mr S. Shepherd, who is unfailing in his efforts to give his patrons a good programme of films from week to week, and in keeping it thoroughly up to date" (BN Feb 26 1915).

Fri Apr 16 1915

The programme of films was replaced by a lecture (illustrated by slides) entitled "Actors and Statesmen" and given by Mr Thomas Cox Meech, in aid of the funds of the Literary and Scientific Institute. A native of Bridport, Meech was a barrister, journalist, Parliamentary lobbyist and newspaper editor.

The first part of his lecture consisted of an account of Parliamentary ceremonial and leading actors, the second "of inimitable mimicry of character, which delighted everybody. His character studies, indeed, were remarkable for the truth and fidelity of their reproduction. Gladstone, Asquith, Churchill, Lloyd George, Tim Healy, Henry Irving, Harry Lauder, and a host of others were made to re-appear in voice and mannerism, and the idea of actors addressing the House as politicians, and statesmen on the stage as actors, each retaining his own individuality, was so excruciatingly funny that the audience at times roared with laughter" (BN Apr 23 1915).

Thu Jun 17 to Sat Jun 19 1915

The programme included Chaplin's 27th Keystone film *The New Janitor* and a set of still views of the 1st Dorset Battery R.F.A. in India, made into slides from photographs sent home by Sergeant A. H. Price.

Tue Sep 7 1915

Fire at the Electric Palace just before the 6.30 p.m. start of the evening's programme, which consisted of *The Million Dollar Mystery, Episode No. 13 – The Secret Agent from Russia*, a special topical film *In the Mine-Strewn North Sea*, and several good Comedy Subjects.

"Through the timely action of the operator and Mr Shepherd, assisted by those living close by, the result was not so serious as it might have been. The ignition tube of the engine exploded, and a particle of the red hot porcelain fell on a piece of rag saturated with oil, and it was in this way the fire originated. Apart from some of the electrical machinery there was not much damage done, and luckily most of the films (which are inflammable) were in their fireproof boxes. The Bridport Fire Brigade were called, and were at the Palace with great promptitude, but the fire was then well under command. The Palace, in consequence, will not be open for a few days, but the necessary repairs will be rectified as soon as possible, and patrons may look forward to their usual evening entertainments without much delay" (BN Sep 10 1915).

In that same issue of the BN there was, instead of the following week's programme, a bald announcement in capitals: The Palace will be closed for a few days only, owing to a breakdown of the electrical installation.

The Palace reopened on Wed Sep 15 1915 with the entertaining Chaplin two-reeler *His New Job* as the main attraction, replaced for the rest of the week by Essanay's latest comedy production in two parts, *Champion Charlie* – a riot of fun with the famous Charles Chaplin.

As the BN Sep 17 1915 noted: "No time has been lost in repairing the damage to the electrical installation done by the fire last week. The work has been carried out under the personal supervision of Mr Shepherd, assisted by Mr Floyd, his chief electrician, from the Littlehampton Palace, and the operator Mr Ryan. Previous to the fire, the Home Secretary's regulations had been carried out to the letter, but now additional measures of protection have been taken, and so far as human ingenuity can provide against it, even a repetition of the experience of last week has been rendered practically impossible."

BN Oct 15 1915

"Owing to the great demand for the famous 'Charles Chaplin' films, Mr Shepherd informs us that they are somewhat difficult to obtain at the moment, but several are booked for the near future, so that patrons of the Palace have a great treat in store for them."

By the end of the year they had been given the chance to see four of his latest Essanay comedies, plus two of the earlier Keystone films. *The Tramp*, generally considered his first real masterpiece, was shown Feb 17–19 1916.

Sat Nov 6 1915

A percentage of the receipts on this Saturday evening were handed to the local committee of the "Our Day" fund, organised by the Red Cross for the British wounded. In the programme was *Getting Acquainted*, starring Chaplin and Mabel Normand.

The following Tuesday (Nov 9) "the Cinema theatres throughout Great Britain gave the whole of that day's takings to a fund to present the Government with fifty motor ambulances etc. for use at the front, and doubtless crowded audiences were the rule; at any rate, our local Palace was full nearly all the evening, and the Management state that the very satisfactory sum of £6 15s was the full takings, and will be handed over without any deduction whatever. The programme presented was a very lengthy one and lasted over three hours. Unfortunately, the principal picture 'When Rome Ruled' did not arrive in time to be shown owing to its having been held up by the Customs Authorities on its return from the Channel Islands, but the substitute 'Tinsel and Tragedy' was a splendid production" (BN Nov 12 1915).

Mr Warren's Orchestra again provided the music during the evening..

BN Dec 10 1915

"During the present dark winter nights a visit to our local Picture Palace cannot fail to bring pleasure and brightness, and drive from the mind for the moment the horrors of the war which is now raging throughout Europe."

Mon Feb 21 to Sat Feb 26 1916 – Fourth Anniversary Week

The special attractions this year were:

Mon–Wed "Pathé's" elaborate and beautifully coloured Masterpiece *Marguerite of Navarre*. A costly adaption (sic) in four parts of the celebrated historical romance "La Reine Margot" by Alexandre Dumas. Settings, Mountings and Scenery of the most luxurious description.

Thu–Sat "Gaumont's" Stupendous Exclusive Production in four parts *The Jockey of Death*. A Magnificent Drama of the circus, in which sensationalism of the most pronounced character is the predominant feature.

The Bridport News annual report on the Palace's progress was, as before, favourable: "We again congratulate Mr Shepherd on another successful year's running of the local Picture Palace, where many hundreds of people have now made their regular visits for their weekly amusements. Despite the war, the audiences continue to be as large as ever, and this is owing to the popularity of the programmes and the good organisation of Mr S. Shepherd, who is always determined to procure the best films for his patrons, and we trust that the Palace will continue to be successful for the future" (BN Feb 25 1916).

This was the last of the special anniversary weeks.

Mon May 15 1916

Up to now the popular prices of admission had remained 3d, 6d and 1s. On this date the new Entertainment Ticket Tax came into force, with the result that the prices (including tax) became 4d, 7d and 1s 2d. Children under 12 were still admitted to the Saturday matinees for 1d and free of tax.

Mon Oct 23 to Wed Oct 25 1916

Showing of *The Battle of the Somme*, a film which had been running for a considerable time at the Scala Theatre, London, and which had recently been seen by the King.

"This film is probably the most wonderful war picture that has ever been exhibited, for the simple reason that many portions of it were taken while the fighting was actually in progress, and its presentation on the screen not only brings home to one what war really means, but it is also calculated to still further increase the admiration which everyone feels for the bravery of our soldiers who are fighting for their country on the battlefield. The War in all its horrors is to be seen, and for the first time we are given the opportunity of realising what those brave soldiers of ours have to go through. The British War Office film is in five parts, and for nearly an hour-and-a-half the audience is shown various stages of the fighting. There are, of course, lighter sides to the picture, but these vanish into mere nothings when that which the film is meant to convey is realised.

A commencement is made by showing troops on their way to the trenches, and in the subsequent stages there are seen guns at work, and the havoc that they bring about. Tons of earthworks are blown into the air, to come down into millions of pieces. The dauntless courage of the British Tommy is vividly portrayed, and, what is even more noticeable, his kindness to a defeated foe. Several examples of this are seen when beaten Germans have surrendered, and in one instance an officer is seen giving a badly wounded enemy refreshment from his bottle, whilst a Tommy comes along with a case of cigarettes.

These are the actions which help to make our fighting men the finest in the world. But as for the picture itself, it will be remembered as one of the remarkable achievements of the cinematograph. As we have said, it shows us war as it really is – war in all its grim and heart-gripping reality. The story of the great triumph for Britain's splendid new armies has never been more graphically told than it is upon this wonderful film. Then the mechanical side of the war is vividly depicted, for the audience see all kinds of guns in the act of bombarding the trenches where the Germans are. Perhaps the most interesting part of the whole picture is that which shows the advance on the 1st of July, and where our men are to be seen going over the top of a trench, headed by their officers. Solemn indeed are the sights of the dead, and another such moment is that when British soldiers are to be seen burying the German dead.

Intensely interesting as the film is as a record of the greatest war in the history of the world, it is as a human document that it will make its strongest and most irresistible appeal to the people. They see their own flesh and blood, these soldiers who march before them, and there are thousands of faces, each of which will be recognised by someone! These pictures were taken under actual fire, and yet the quality and detail is perfect! Think what risks the brave men who secured them must have run, in order that we at home might be able to see for ourselves what present-day warfare means.

As there will be large audiences at each performance, we strongly advise our readers to book in advance. Please note times:- Matinees each day at 3, and two shows each night at 6 and 8.30" (BN Oct 20 1916).

The BN Oct 27 1916 reported that "at each of the three performances given each day the Palace was crowded with appreciative audiences".

The Battle of the Somme, an offensive intended to relieve pressure on the French at Verdun, began on Jul 1 1916, when some 20,000 British soldiers were killed. By Nov 18 the allies had advanced ten miles and lost 600,000 men, two-thirds of them British. Tanks were used for the first time by the British on Sept 15.

BN Dec 22 1916

"The manager of the Palace, Mr S. Shepherd shortly leaves Bridport to join the colours, and in his absence, the management will be undertaken by the Misses Shepherd, who will continue to 'carry on' this popular house of entertainment as successfully as in the past."

The Misses Shepherd were Rose and Daisy, the former later becoming Mrs George Knight of the Bull Hotel. Throughout this interim period of female control the weekly advertisements in the BN continued to state that the manager was Sydney C. Shepherd.

Wed Feb 14 1917

A Grand Musical Evening, arranged by Mr Frank P. Spicer, was held at the Palace under the patronage of Col. Downing, DSO, and J. C. Palmer, Esq., Mayor, in aid of the Soldiers' Club and the Soldiers' Comforts Fund. Many high-class professional artistes, now members of the Training Reserve, took part. The Regimental orchestra was conducted by Mrs Alexander, who also provided the plants on the platform. Seats were 2s (reserved), 1s and 6d.

Thu May 10 to Sat May 12 1917

Included in the programme: The National Egg Collection Film – *From Hen to Hospital*. Don't Miss this Extremely Interesting Film, and so Help our Gallant Wounded Soldiers and Sailors.

The national scheme for collecting new-laid eggs for wounded soldiers and sailors in hospital had come into operation in West Dorset in late March 1915, eggs from the surrounding parishes being sent to Bridport Town Hall on Wednesdays.

At the end of Feb 1919 another film was shown for three days in aid of the funds for the National Egg Collection for the Wounded: *The Love That Lasts*. An Egg Story. Collections were made at each performance.

Thu Jun 7 to Sat Jun 9 1917

Included in the programme: The Greatest Naval Picture Ever Shown – *For the Honour of Australia* – an Official Film by special permission of the British and Australian Admiralties.

"This picture has as its central figures two orphan boys, one of whom joins the Australian Navy, and on the outbreak of war is drafted to the Sydney, while the other, a ne'er-do-well, helps his country in another way, and, aided by a young Maori girl, first destroys a secret wireless installation of the enemy and afterwards assists the crew of the Sydney to finally break up a band of German spies. Some excellent scenes of the Australian Navy leaving harbour at the outbreak of hostilities and of the sadly battered Emden after her encounter with the Sydney are introduced, but the most exciting episode of the story is how the young Maori girl eventually gives her life for the honour of Australia" (BN Jun 8 1917). Any New Zealander would, of course, do the same.

A German version of the story of the light cruiser Emden was shown in March 1928 at the Palace in South Street.

Mon Oct 1 1917

The Increased Entertainment Tax came into force. The price of each ticket – including tax – went up by 1d to 5d, 8d and 1s 3d.

Mon Dec 3 to Wed Dec 5 1917

Sarah Bernhardt, who had had her right leg amputated in Feb 1915, could be seen in the morale-boosting *Jeanne Doré*, made late in 1915. In this film she played in over a hundred scenes either sitting or standing still.

Mon Jan 14 1918

A special cinema lantern lecture was held in the Palace at 2.30 p.m., with pictures relating to the patriotic national work done by old Dr Barnado boys. These were stills, not moving pictures as was originally announced (BN Jan 11 1918). The cinema was lent free for this event, and the collection taken for Dr Barnado's Homes amounted to £9 10s.

Mon Jan 28 to Wed Jan 30 1918

Included in the programme: *Her Greatest Performance*, starring Ellen Terry. "Introducing the 'Queen of the English Stage' for the first time to Cinema Audiences. A diverting story showing how a great actress used her acting power in order to save her son from a wrongful conviction.

The picture of which a Command Performance was given before Queen Alexandra."

This was the first of Ellen Terry's five fairly ineffective film appearances – she was 70 at the time.

Mon Jun 24 to Wed Jun 26 1918

Included in the programme: Mr H. Sykes, Britain's Most Intrepid Airman (by kind permission of Mr J. A. Whitehead of the Whitehead Aircraft Co.) in *A Munition Girl's Romance*. The Great Broadwest Production in Four Parts. A Highly attractive Film at the present time. Several of the Scenes give a realistic portrayal of the interior of one of our leading Aircraft Factories Working at Wartime pressure. PATRONS SHOULD NOT MISS THIS.

This film would appear to be comparable to Launder and Gilliat's excellent *Millions Like Us* (1943) about girls working in an aircraft factory in the Second World War.

Bank Holiday Mon Aug 4 1918

"On Monday evening Mr E. J. Wotton Buckpitt read the Prime Minister's message to the nation at the Electric Picture Palace, when it was received with patriotic applause by the crowded audience. Attractive film displays have brought big houses this week, and on Monday it was at times almost impossible to obtain even standing room. The chief pictures were a delightful Hepworth photo-play, 'Merely Mrs Stubbs', and the famous comedian Lupino Lane was seen at his best in 'Splash Me Nicely'" (BN Aug 9 1918).

The Premier's message to the British Empire was read out in every theatre, every cinema and every place of public meeting where Bank Holiday crowds were assembled. Its text was as follows:

10, Downing Street,
S.W.1.

The message which I send to the people of the British Empire on the fourth anniversary of their entry into the war is "Hold Fast".

We are in this war for no selfish ends. We are in it to recover freedom for the nations which have been brutally attacked and despoiled, and to prove that no people, however powerful, can surrender itself to the lawless ambitions of militarism without meeting retribution, swift, certain, and disastrous, at the hands of the free nations of the world. To stop short of victory for this cause would be to compromise the future of mankind.

I say "Hold Fast", because our prospects of victory have never been so bright as they are today. Six months ago the rulers of Germany deliberately rejected the just and reasonable settlement proposed by the Allies. Throwing aside the last mask of moderation, they partitioned Russia, enslaved Roumania, and attempted to seize supreme power by overwhelming the Allies in a final and desperate attack. Thanks to the invincible bravery of all the Allied armies it is now evident to all that this dream of universal conquest, for the sake of which they wantonly prolonged the war, can never be fulfilled.

But the battle is not yet won. The great autocracy of Prussia will still endeavour by violence or guile to avoid defeat and so give militarism a new lease of life. We cannot seek to escape the horrors of war for ourselves by laying them up for our children. Having set our hands to the task we must see it through till a just and lasting settlement is achieved.

In no other way can we ensure a world set free from war.

Hold Fast!

Aug 4, 1918   D. LLOYD GEORGE

August to December 1918

In these five months all 12 of the almost perfect two-reel comedies Chaplin made in 1916 and 1917 for the Mutual Co. – at ten times his 1915 salary – were shown at the Palace:

August	*The Floorwalker; The Fireman; The Count*
September	*The Pawnship; Behind the Screen*
October	*One a.m.; The Vagabond; The Rink*
November	*Easy Street* (for the first weekend of peace); *The Cure*
December	*The Immigrant; The Adventurer; The Rink* (again, immediately after Christmas).

More than half of these films were revived throughout 1923.

Mon Mar 24 to Sat Mar 29 1919

The cinema was closed for necessary decorations.

Previously the weekly BN advertisement had indicated that the manager was Mr Shepherd. From Mar 28 1919 he became "resident manager". This addition of "resident" at this point suggests that he had now returned to Bridport after war service and taken over the reins of management from his sisters.

Mon Jul 7 to Wed Jul 9 1919

Included in the programme: Chaplin's *Shoulder Arms*, a two-reel war comedy, set in the trenches, in which Charlie dreams of defeating the Kaiser single-handedly. This was his most popular success to date, particularly amongst the troops and ex-servicemen.

In the latter part of the week patrons could see *Our Boys in Germany*, the Thrilling Official Photographs of the Daily Life of Our Lads now keeping the Watch on the Rhine, and a month later a special film of the *Victory March Through London*, which had taken place on Jul 19.

Thu Nov 20 to Wed Nov 26 1919 (excluding Sunday)

Private J. H. W. Porter of the National Institute for the Blind and St Dunstan's presented each evening at 8 p.m. the great picture *St Dunstan's*, "showing our Blinded Heroes at Work and at Play". In the advertisement in the BN Nov 21 1919 Pte Porter publicly thanked Mr Shepherd for the splendid patriotic spirit he had displayed in giving his permission for this event at the Palace. Prices remained unchanged – there was no extra charge for the extra attraction.

Private Porter was visiting Bridport in order to organise a six-week funding effort on behalf of his blinded comrades.

Eleven days later St Dunstan's Effort in Bridport arranged for the film *If Thou Wert Blind* to be exhibited at the Electric Palace on Sun Dec 7 at 8.15 p.m.

Collections at the cinema amounted to £16 13s 7³/₄d.

BN Feb 27 1920

A change in the prices of admission: the more expensive seats went up to 9d and 1/6, but the cheapest seats remained at 5d (including tax).

Mon Apr 12 to Wed Apr 14 1920

"Secured at great expense and after long negotiation, Mary Pickford in her greatest success *Daddy Longlegs*." In it the World's Sweetheart played an orphan who finds happiness with her benefactor – a typical sweet, innocent, "Little Mary" role, which Janet Gaynor and Leslie Caron were to play later, in 1931 and 1955 respectively.

Other Pickford films shown at the Electric Palace include *In a Bishop's Carriage* (4/15); *Captain Kidd Junior* (7/19); *Johanna Enlists* (10/19); *The Ragamuffin* (5/22), better known as *Suds*; *Heart o'the Hills* (7/22); *Little Lord Fauntleroy* (2/23), in which she plays the boy and his mother; *Tess of the Storm Country* (10/24).

BN Jun 4 1920

"We need not fear the future of British cinematography all the time the Broadwest Company continue to furnish us with such admirable films as 'In the Gloaming', featuring Violet Hopson. This picture, which was the chief attraction during the earlier part of the week, was made doubly successful by the charming singing of Miss Hilda Crabbe, the popular pianist at the Palace, who introduced the song during the screening of the story with marked effect, and brought expressions of appreciation from each successive audience."

BN Jun 18 1920

"Mr Shepherd informs us he has made arrangements to take a film of tomorrow's Carnival. A first-class camera man has been secured at great expense, and is being sent down from London, returning the same night to enable the film to be developed on Sunday, and sent to Bridport in time for exhibition on Monday evening. It will be kept in the programme the whole of next week, and Mr Shepherd deserves crowded houses every night as a reward for his enterprise."

"Alexandra Day in Bridport. Our Film of the Carnival" was duly shown. Queen Alexandra had inaugurated Alexandra Rose Day in aid of hospitals in June 1912 to celebrate the 50th year of her residence in England.

Two years later in the BN Aug 4 1922 the Palace management announced that a film of the Carnival would be taken on Mon Aug 7, "so look out for the camera and get included in the picture". The film was in the programme from Wed Aug 9 and continued until Wed Aug 16. It reappeared for three days "by request of numerous patrons" in mid-July 1923.

Mon Oct 25 to Wed Oct 27 1920

Tarzan of the Apes was given two separate performances each day at 5.45 and 8.15. There was to be a special matinee on the Wednesday, but this, along with a children's matinee on the previous Saturday, was cancelled "owing to the restrictions in the gas supply".

On the three evenings "there were crowded audiences at the Electric Palace, drawn by the special attraction of one of the most wonderful films ever produced and known as the wonder film of the age" (BN Oct 29 1920).

Its sequel *The Romance of Tarzan* was shown the following week (Nov 1–3).

Edgar Rice Burroughs' first Tarzan novel, "Tarzan of the Apes", had been published in 1914, and these two films, with Elmo Lincoln as the jungle hero and Enid Markey as Jane, were made four years later. The first sound film version – and arguably the best of all the Tarzan films – was *Tarzan the Ape Man*, made in 1932 and starring Johnny Weissmuller and Maureen O'Sullivan. It was shown at the Palace in South Street at the end of December 1932.

Mon Nov 8 to Wed Nov 19 1920

The main attraction in the programme was *The Romance of Lady Hamilton*, the Romantic Life History of the "MOTHER OF THE BRITISH NAVY".

It would be interesting to compare this film and Malvina Longfellow's performance as Emma with Alexander Korda's 1941 version of the affair with Vivien Leigh and Laurence Olivier.

Mon Nov 29 to Wed Dec 1 1920

Although the main film was an attractive Swedish production *Dawn of Love*, starring one of the most gifted and cultured actresses of the Swedish stage, Harriet Bosse, the outstanding item in the programme was considered to be the film of the Burial of the Unknown Warrior and the Unveiling of the Cenotaph by the King, events which had taken place on Nov 11 1920. "A very interesting and impressive picture was splendidly accompanied with very suitable music by the popular pianiste, Mrs Thear" (BN Dec 3 1920).

BN Apr 22 1921

The Palace management announced the showing for three days (Apr 25–27) of *Eye for an Eye*, the first of a series of five masterpieces featuring the new sensation of the screen Nazimova, the World's Greatest Emotional Actress. What the other four were remains uncertain, as there were no further cinema advertisements in the BN throughout 1921, apart from the Christmas issue. Normal service resumed in March 1922.

Thu Jan 19 to Sat Jan 21 1922

Showing of Chaplin's first feature-length film, in six reels: *The Kid*, with child star Jackie Coogan. There was an extra performance for children at 11 o'clock on Saturday morning; it was only to this performance that they were admitted at half price.

The Kid had taken 18 months to film and cost half a million dollars, but it proved to be more profitable than any movie made up to that time (1921), with the exception of D. W. Griffith's *The Birth of a Nation*. Chaplin's second feature *The Pilgrim*, almost as popular, reached Bridport in Jan 1924.

Thu Feb 9 to Sat Feb 11 1922

Showing of *The True Story of the Battle of Jutland*, based on British and German logs, with a script by Major-General Sir George Ashton K.C.B. Made for British Instructional Films using documentary material and animated maps and diagrams, this was the first of a series of reconstructions of various engagements of the First World War, including Ypres, Mons, the Somme and the battles of the Coronel and Falkland Islands.

From the BN Sep 15 1922 to its closure the cinema advertised as The Palace, Bridport.

Thu Aug 17 to Sat Aug 19 1922

Showing of *Among Those Present*, the first of a series of three-reel comedies featuring Harold Lloyd, "the Comedian who has come to the front with a jump". It was followed at the Palace by *I Do* (Sep), *Never Weaken* (Oct, advertised as *Don't Weaken*) and *Now or Never* (Nov).

"Harold Lloyd (formerly known as 'Winkle') is the only comedian who inspires real healthy laughter without the aid of comedy clothes, burlesque make-up or slapstick business, and his comedies are always a success because all his funny situations are predicaments that might happen to any of us" (BN Aug 18 1922). A few of these earlier films, in which he played a mild-mannered, bespectacled character named Winkle, were shown at the Palace in 1920 (Aug–Sep), and later on all his main silent features came to Barrack Street: *A Sailor-Made Man* (5/23), *Grandma's Boy* (7/23), *Dr Jack* (6/24, advertised as *Doctor's Orders*), *Safety Last* (8/24), *Why Worry?* (9/24), *Girl Shy* (4/25), *College Days/The Freshman* (4/26, one of the most successful of all silent films).

Noted for his dangerous stunts, Lloyd rivalled Chaplin and Keaton in popularity during the 1920s and indeed surpassed them at the American box office.

Mon Nov 13 to Wed Nov 15 1922

Included in the programme: Louise Glaum in her greatest triumph SEX. A highly interesting and logical story startling in originality and effectiveness, with lavish production.

Miss Glaum wears no fewer than 24 gowns during the unfolding of the story.

Clearly this film had something to offer both male and female patrons of the Palace. Louise Glaum usually played a Theda Bara style "vamp" and seductively tempted the unsmiling William S. Hart in dozens of Westerns during this period.

Thu Nov 23 to Sat Nov 25 1922

Showing of D. W. Griffiths's *True Heart Susie*, a charming rustic romance starring the talented Lillian Gish. She and her sister Dorothy were to be seen two years later in Griffith's impressive *Orphans of the Storm* (Nov 27–29 1924). Neither of his most celebrated films – *The Birth of a Nation* (1915) and *Intolerance* (1916) – seems to have found its way to Bridport.

Thu Dec 7 to Sat Dec 9 1922

Sessue Hayakawa in one of his greatest successes *Where Lights are Low*. A thrilling love story of the Chinese underworld, permeated with all the mysterious charm of oriental tradition.

Hayakawa was a popular Japanese actor who appeared in several Hollywood films between 1914 and 1923. He is best remembered now for his portrayal of the prison camp commandant in *The Bridge on the River Kwai*, shown at the Palace, South Street, in May 1958, Aug 1963 and Feb 1968.

At the beginning of the following week Palace patrons could see Madame Réjane, the wonderful and famous French actress, in *Miarka – the Child of the Bear*, from the novel by Jean Richepin – a French triumph of artistic production and wonderful acting, recently shown at Marlborough House by request of H.M. Queen Alexandra. (Réjane had died in 1920 in her early 60s.) Then Dec 18–20 there was *Payment in Full*, a beautiful Italian production starring Signorina Manzini.

At this time it was obviously possible for Bridport audiences to see and enjoy without difficulty films not only from America and Britain but also from Europe, in particular France, Italy, Sweden and Denmark (the Nordisk Film Company). Once the talkies came, English-language films inevitably monopolized the programmes, and it was not until the advent of the X certificate in 1951 that Continental films returned in any number to the Bridport screens.

Mon Mar 19 to Wed Mar 21 1923

Showing of "the wonder film of the Arctic Nanook of the North
The Picture that is different.
The Picture that all must see."

Robert Flaherty's fine documentary on Eskimo life, in five reels, had received its London première in early September 1922. Re-issued in July 1947 in a sound version, the film reappeared, appropriately, at the Lyric for three days May 12–14 1949.

Mon Apr 23 to Wed Apr 25 1923

A different big picture each night: on Monday De Mille's *The Woman God Forgot* (1917), starring the American opera singer Geraldine Farrar – on Tuesday *Barbary*

Sheep (1917), with Elsie Ferguson – on Wednesday *The Career of Katherine Bush* (1919), with Catherine Calvert, from a novel by Elinor Glyn. The advertisement added a note to explain this unusual programming: "The demand for these three beautiful productions has been so great that they can on no account be retained for a longer period."

Mon Aug 20 to Wed Aug 22 1923

Supporting *Five Days to Live*, with Sessue Hayakawa, was *The Playhouse*, a two-reeler starring the greatest of the silent film clowns Buster Keaton. This was followed by several more of his outstanding short comedies, including *The Paleface* (8/23), *Cops* (11/23), in which Buster is joined by about 300 policemen, *The Electric House* (1/25), *The Love Nest* (1/25) and *The Balloonatic* (5/25). Between 1923 and 1928 he made ten features, including *Our Hospitality*, *Sherlock Junior*, *The Navigator* and *Seven Chances*, which were all shown in Barrack Street between Oct 1924 and Mar 1926.

Mon Sep 24 to Wed Sep 26 1923

Showing of *The Sheik*, one of Rudolph Valentino's most successful films, "a photoplay of tempestuous love between a madcap English beauty and a bronzed Arab chief!"

By 1921 Valentino had become a great romantic idol, and his films appeared regularly in the Palace's programmes, e.g. *The Conquering Power* (5/23), a version of Balzac's "Eugénie Grandet"; *Beyond the Rocks* (12/23), with Gloria Swanson, from a novel by Elinor Glyn; *The Four Horsemen of the Apocalypse* (3/24); *Frivolous Wives* (2/25); *Monsieur Beaucaire* (10–15/8/25); *A Sainted Devil* (1/26).

The Mexican Ramon Novarro was launched as a Latin lover in 1922, but was somewhat overshadowed by Valentino. In July 1924 he was seen at the Palace in Rex Ingram's *Where the Pavement Ends*, with Alice Terry, then in *Scaramouche* (5/25) and *The Arab* (7/25), but his greatest success was to come with *Ben Hur*.

Mon Oct 22 to Wed Oct 24 1923

Enormous Attraction Secured at Great Expense – *The Queen of Sheba* – The world's greatest love story. There were two separate performances each evening at 6 and 8.20, with Monday and Wednesday matinees at 2.15. Prices were increased to 6d, 1/-, 1/10.

This American epic involved 10,000 people, 500 horses and camels and cost over £200,000. The chariot race in it was supervised by the popular cowboy star Tom Mix. The title role was played by Betty Blythe who remarked: "I wear twenty-eight costumes, and if I put them all on at once, I couldn't keep warm." She can be seen as one of Doolittle's cronies in the film of *My Fair Lady* (1964).

Accompanying *The Queen of Sheba* were First Pictures of the Japanese Earthquake Disaster, i.e. that of Sep 1 1923 when Tokyo and Yokohama were destroyed with 156,000 dead.

Mon Dec 10 1923

A Benefit Performance in aid of the Mayor's Christmas Fund was given, just three days after the Mayor, Mr W. E. Bates, had announced the setting up of the Fund in a letter to the Bridport News. In a further letter, published in the BN Dec 14 and dated Dec 12, the Mayor wrote: "I should like publicly to acknowledge the receipt of £10 2s

10d from Mr Sydney Shepherd, the proceeds of the Benefit Performance he so kindly gave on Monday last at the Picture Palace."

The main film that evening was a fine British drama *Mr Wu*, from one of the most successful plays the country has ever seen. It starred Matheson Lang in his most famous role – indeed he called his autobiography "Mr Wu Looks Back".

After the performances on Wed Dec 19 1923 the cinema did not reopen until Boxing Day.

Mon Mar 3 to Sat Mar 8 1924

The first feature film to be given a week's run: Rex Ingram's wonderful production, direct from seven months' continuous run at the Palace Theatre, London, starring Rudolph Valentino and Alice Terry, *The Four Horsemen of the Apocalypse*. Presented with realistic effects at each performance. This remarkable 2¼-hour film of Blasco Ibanez's best-selling novel about brothers fighting on opposite sides in the recent world war had been released in New York on Mar 6 1921 and made Valentino a star – the sequence in which he dances the tango had the ladies swooning in the aisles.

Two separate and distinct performances were given each evening at 5.30 and 8.30. There were special matinees on Mon, Wed, Thu and Sat, and special prices: 6d, 1/-, 1/10, including War Tax. Children full price to all performances. However, a limited number of children (under 12) were admitted at 3d each at the final matinee on Saturday.

Immediately following this American triumph was a British Film Week:

Mon–Wed *The School for Scandal*, starring Queenie Thomas, plus a charming little picture in Pathecolor *The Story of the Nightingale*

Thu–Sat *Guy Fawkes*, with the popular Matheson Lang, a stage actor-manager who regularly appeared in films from 1916 to the mid-1930s.

Mon May 26 to Wed Jun 4 1924

For these ten days the cinema was closed. When it reopened on Jun 5 with Harold Lloyd in *Doctor's Orders* (better known as *Dr Jack*), there were new prices of admission: 4d, 8d, 1/3, including tax, i.e. a reduction of 1d, 1d and 3d respectively. Children under 12 half price only when accompanied by adults. Full price Saturday nights and Bank Holidays. At matinees children (under 12) 2d to front seats; over that age full price.

BN Dec 19 1924

"The Mayor and Mayoress (Mr and Mrs F. Weeks) attended a special performance at the Picture Palace on Tuesday evening when, through the kindness of Mr Sydney C. Shepherd, the proprietor, the whole of the proceeds, less tax, were given to the Mayor's Christmas fund. The film, 'The Eternal City' by Sir Hall Caine, proved a strong attraction, and the building was filled with a large and appreciative audience. An excellent musical programme was provided, songs being rendered by Mrs T. H. Thear, Miss Mildred Perrott and Mr J. Reed, while in addition monologues were given by Mr Pennock, and selections discoursed by Mr W. J. Stoodley's syncopated band. The Mayor during an interval thanked Mr Shepherd for his generosity, the artistes who had kindly given their services, and the public for the support accorded to the fund.

We are pleased to announce that a cheque for £11 8s 2d has been handed to the Mayor."

One of the attractions of *The Eternal City*, shown on that Tue Dec 16, was the presence of the sultry and beautiful Barbara La Marr.

Fri Jan 30 1925

The Palace was let to the White Star Shipping Company on this evening for an illustrated cinema and lantern lecture on "Canada, and what it has to offer", given by Mr O. Thery (Representative of the White Star Line) – "a lecture that should prove of great interest to all who have the cause of Empire at heart" – and who were thinking of emigrating at the time. Admission was free.

Further encouragement to the faint-hearted was conveniently provided the following day, for the programme included a special RNLI film entitled *Over 58,000 Lives Saved*. A collection was taken at each performance.

Thu Feb 26 to Sat Feb 28 1925

Showing of *The Romance of a Queen*, Elinor Glyn's production of her famous 1907 novel "Three Weeks", starring Aileen Pringle and Conrad Nagel. This was the story of a young aristocratic Englishman seduced by a passionate Slavonic beauty so that she could present her royal husband with an heir. When the novel was published it shocked society with its erotic scenes played out on a tiger-skin, became a best-seller and was translated into nearly every European language. The film was considered daring for its sexual frankness and may well have raised a few eyebrows in Bridport in 1925.

Thu Mar 5 to Wed Mar 11 1925 (excluding Sunday)

Showing of an impressive, if simplified, version of *The Hunchback of Notre Dame*, with Lon Chaney as Quasimodo. Not quite as good as Charles Laughton in 1939, but superior to the Disney vision of Hugo's novel.

Fri Mar 13 1925

The cinema was lent to the Society for the Propagation of the Gospel for the showing of a film on Burma, with a descriptive lecture by Mr J. T. Best. This event began at 2.30 p.m., tickets cost 2/- and 1/-, with all proceeds going to the S.P.G.

Mon Apr 6 to Sat Apr 11 1925 (excluding Good Friday)

Showing of the British film *Reveille* – the story of a Month in 1918 and a Month in 1923. "This picture will be presented at every performance with Bugle Calls and Special Effects." It starred Stewart Rome and Betty Balfour, one of Britain's most popular silent film comediennes.

Mon May 18 to Wed May 27 1925

The Palace was closed for its annual spring cleaning.

Thu Sep 3 to Wed Sep 9 1925 (excluding Sunday)

Showing of Cecil B. De Mille's spectacular *The Ten Commandments*. Its imminent arrival had been announced by an extra large advertisement in the BN Aug 28 1925, which included the following description:

"An entertainment not of the passing moment but of all time.

True of the past – True in the present – True of the future.

The dead splendours of past civilisations live again in vivid scenes with natural colours.

The achievements and weaknesses of today are contrasted as in a picture painted by a master-hand.

And through all is woven a story that will delight you by its beauty and inspire you by its message."

Unlike the 1956 remake, which confines itself to the biblical story, this first 1923 version adds a modern tale of contemporary Americans who have forsaken the Mosaic tenets. It was shown twice nightly at 5.45 and 8.15, with a 2 p.m. Saturday matinee. As had happened for *The Queen of Sheba*, *The Four Horsemen of the Apocalypse* and *The Hunchback of Notre Dame*, prices were raised to 6d, 1/- and 1/10 – children full price at all performances.

The remake in VistaVision, with Charles Heston, Yul Brynner, Edward G. Robinson, Anne Baxter and Yvonne De Carlo, was shown at the Palace, South Street, for ten days in the second half of May 1960, and for another five days in the first half of May 1967.

Wed Nov 11 1925

A Benefit Performance in aid of the British Legion's Poppy Fund was given, with a specially augmented programme. There was a brief report of the occasion in the BN Nov 13 1925 under the heading PICTURE PALACE: "At this place of amusement on Wednesday the whole of the takings less tax were given to Earl Haig's fund for disabled ex-Servicemen. An excellent musical programme was rendered by Draper's orchestra, and vocal items were given by Mr Hutchings' quartette, Mr and Mrs T. Thear and Mr Baker. During the interval Mr F. E. Page, the hon. secretary of the Bridport branch of the British Legion, thanked Mr S. Shepherd (proprietor) for his generosity and the artistes who had contributed to the programme."

The main film that evening was *The Lady*, starring Norma Talmadge – a Drama of Mother Love reaching from poverty's depths to Society's heights.

Mon Nov 16 to Wed Nov 18 1925

Showing of *The Covered Wagon*, the first great epic Western, shot entirely on location and eclipsing the "old-fashioned" Westerns of William S. Hart.

Wed Dec 9 1925

"The annual benefit performance in aid of the Mayor's Christmas Fund took place at the Palace, Bridport, on Wednesday night, thanks to the renewed generosity of the Proprietor, Mr S. C. Shepherd. The performance which was continuous from six to ten was very largely attended, and the amount raised on behalf of the fund was £8 1s 6d. In addition to the all-British film 'The Happy Ending' featuring Fay Compton and Jack Buchanan, a number of local artistes very generously contributed towards the programme including songs by Mr J. Reed and Mr F. Trevett and an amusing recitation in the Devonshire dialect by Mrs Leaker. The Mayor and Mayoress (Mr and Mrs F. Weeks) were present and during the course of the evening the Mayor extended his thanks to the artistes and also to Mr Shepherd" (BN Dec 11 1925).

Mon Jan 18 to Wed Jan 20 1926

Included in the programme: The Screen's Latest Novelty *Plastigrams* – A film of stereoscopic pictures producing positively startling effects with the aid of patent spectacles loaned free of charge at each performance. A second *Plastigrams* film was shown Feb 18–20 1926.

These shorts were released by Paramount, but this anaglyph process was ultimately found to be unsatisfactory as the picture remained somewhat indistinct and the spectacles caused headaches. That these experimental films were shown at the Palace is much to the credit of Mr Shepherd, who was always prepared to keep Bridport abreast of current cinematic developments and successes (see Jun 9–10 1953).

Thu Jan 21 to Sat Jan 23 1926

With *Felix the Cat Trifles With Time* in the programme there was a Felix Limerick Competition – Ideal Films Ltd offered prizes of £3, £2, £1 each fortnight for the best limerick last line. Full particulars were handed to all patrons as they took their tickets of admission.

BN Apr 30 1926

For the first time the advertisement offered some useful transport information: "Special late 'Buses leave for Beaminster (Service 22a), Bowood only (Service 22b), Morcombelake (Service 38), and West Bay after the Performance every Saturday Night."

This notice did not reappear the following week, but in the BN May 14 1926 patrons were informed that "the National 'Buses run a special late service, and Mr Smith's Burton Bradstock 'Bus runs an early and late service every Saturday evening".

Mon May 3 to Wed May 12 1926 – The General Strike

The Palace's programmes were only slightly affected by the strike. The BN May 7 1926 was able to assure cinemagoers that "all evening performances at the Picture Palace will continue as usual, but Saturday's matinee is cancelled".

The main films over these ten days were:

May 3–5 *Wages of Virtue*, from the Famous Novel by Percival Wren, with Gloria Swanson as the girl who becomes the toast of the Foreign Legion

May 6–8 *Steele of the Royal Mounted*, starring Bert Lytell

May 10–12 The Love Story of David *Livingstone* – A Film more Romantic in its making than any Motion-Picture yet produced. A British Masterpiece.

Sat May 29 1926

The Palace closed just over a fortnight before the opening of the New Electric Palace in South Street, which was to be managed by the experienced 41-year-old Sydney C. Shepherd.

The last feature film to be shown was *Siege* (US 1925), "a screen epic of matrimony's lights and shadows", starring Virginia Valli and Eugene O'Brien in a story which "deals with real people, and unflinchingly exposes the problems of modern day marriage". Also in the programme was *Felix Flirts With Fate*.

Thu May 12 1927

To mark the re-opening of the Liberal Hall and Club, the Bridport Liberal Association held a public meeting in the Hall – with a concert and dance on the following evening.

The building had been completely restored and renovated at a cost of £300. Besides the main hall seating about 400, there was a reading room, a spacious billiard room and cloakrooms.

"Until a comparatively recent date the hall was used as a cinema, but many years ago it was the old Congregational Chapel, the pulpit of which is now in the Chapel at Salwayash" (BN May 13 1927).

In addition to the actors and actresses already mentioned, the following – all fairly well known at the time – appeared in films at the Electric Palace in Barrack Street during this period:

Agnes Ayres, Leah Baird, Bessie Barriscale, Lionel Barrymore, Wallace Beery, Enid Bennett, Clive Brook, Billie Burke, Syd Chaplin, Ethel Clayton, Ruth Clifford, Ronald Colman, Betty Compson, Dorothy Dalton, Viola Dana, Bebe Daniels, Marion Davies, Priscilla Dean, Marguerite De La Motte, Dorothy Devore, Henry Edwards, Isobel Elsom, Douglas Fairbanks, Pauline Frederick, Hoot Gibson, John Gilbert, Corinne Griffith, William Haines, Creighton Hale, Kenneth Harlan, Glenn Hunter, Doris Kenyon, Warren Kerrigan, Laura La Plante, Rod La Rocque, Bessie Love, May McAvoy, Mae Marsh, Thomas Meighan, Adolphe Menjou, Tom Mix, Colleen Moore, Carmel Myers, Pola Negri, Anna Q. Nilsson, Jane Novak, Ivor Novello, Tyrone Power Snr, Billie Rhodes, Lillian Rich, Rin-Tin-Tin, Alma Rubens, Monroe Salisbury ("the Irving of the Films"), Milton Sills, Anita Stewart, Lewis Stone, Blanche Sweet, Constance Talmadge, Estelle Taylor, Ernest Torrence, Gladys Walton, Fannie Ward, Chrissie White, Lois Wilson, Clara Kimball Young.

The Lyric Cinema, Barrack Street

Monday December 17 1934 to Saturday September 1 1962

Bridport News Dec 14 1934

Announcement of a Grand Opening on Monday, December 17th of The Lyric, Bridport's New Luxury Cinema – sole proprietress: Mrs M. Weight. There was no mention of those who were behind the venture, Messrs H. Stevenson and Church. (However, in the 1939 edition of Kelly's Directory of Dorsetshire Harry Stevenson has replaced Mrs M. Weight in the Lyric Cinema entry.)

"The new Lyric Theatre in Barrack Street proves what a transformation can be accomplished by adopting modern methods in decorative schemes. The old Liberal Hall has been altered into a cosy up-to-date cinema with every comfort, combined with the latest type projectors and talkie equipment.

The internal decorations are the work of Lawrie Canton, who has to his credit the decorations of the Royal Ballroom at Ascot, the Cosmo Club, London, and many others in Britain and the Continent."

The cinema occupied the lower portion of the Liberal Hall, the upper floor being set aside as headquarters of the West Dorset Liberal Party.

The 1930s were the heyday of the great Hollywood studios, while in this country in the years 1935, 1936, 1937 the British film industry produced more films than at any other period in its history. That the opening of a second cinema in Bridport at this time should be a commercially viable enterprise is, therefore, not altogether surprising.

Mon Dec 17 1934

The Lyric opened with *Paddy the Next Best Thing* (US 1933), the adventures of an Irish tomboy in New York, a 75-min b/w comedy starring Janet Gaynor and Warner Baxter, "a picture which many in the district have been eagerly anticipating".

For the latter part of this first week the main film was *Bottoms Up* (US 1934), an 85-min b/w musical with a Hollywood background, starring Spencer Tracy and John Boles.

Seat prices: 6d, 9d, 1/- and 1/6. Matinee on Saturday at 2.30 – prices for matinee only: 2d, 4d and 6d.

The Palace's double feature programmes that week offered stiff competition despite higher admission prices: 7d, 1/-, 1/6, 2/-. The main attractions were Mon–Wed: *Autumn Crocus* (GB 1934), starring Ivor Novello, Fay Compton and Jack Hawkins; and Thu–Sat: *Berkeley Square* (US 1933), a charming romantic fantasy with Leslie Howard and Heather Angel. The launch, however, was successful, as the BN Dec 21 1934 reported:

"This week has witnessed the opening of Bridport's new cinema, The Lyric, and the expectations of the management, we are assured, have been more than realised by the size of the 'houses'. The arrangements made to ensure the comfort of patrons have received favourable comment, and the programme has been greatly enjoyed. A modern decorative scheme has been carried out by Mr Lawrie Carton, and the seating arrangements are in good taste. Projection and sound system are both excellent, while the heating arrangements, entrusted to Bridport Gas Company, are in every way commendable."

The BN appears to be a little uncertain as to the surname of the decorator.

29

From Dec 27 1935 to Feb 28 1936 the Lyric in its advertisements regularly described itself as being "where everybody goes". A few other slogans were tried during 1936: Lyric Ensures Satisfaction; Lyric – the Rendezvous of Discriminating Picture Goers; 'Tis not in mortals to command success, but we'll do more – deserve it – ADDISON; The Lyric Delivers "The Goods"; Only the very Best is good enough for OUR patrons; You get 100% entertainment at the Lyric; At the Lyric – it's cool or cosy, according to the weather; Lyric Patrons *Are* Right.

With the outbreak of war on Sunday Sep 3 1939 all cinemas were closed. In the BN of Sep 8 the Lyric announced that: "THIS CINEMA IS TEMPORARILY CLOSED and Patrons are asked to watch this space for an announcement of the date of Re-opening" – slightly more optimistic than the management (still Sydney Chas Shepherd) of the Electric Palace, who informed their patrons that "this Cinema will remain closed until further Notice".

The last show at the Lyric in peacetime consisted of *While New York Sleeps* (a "B" picture now sunk without trace), and *Mr Moto's Last Warning*, starring Peter Lorre and dealing with a plot to start a world war by mining the French Fleet when it comes to join the British Fleet at Port Said for combined manoeuvres. Mr Moto, of course, unlike Mr Chamberlain, managed to avert disaster.

Cinemas in the reception and neutral areas were allowed to open again until 10 p.m. from Sep 9.

The Lyric resumed on Sep 11 with the programme already planned for the previous week, i.e. Mon–Wed: *Up the River* (US 1938), a comedy about three convicts, and *Road Demon*; Thu–Sat: *Valley of the Giants* (US 1938), a 79-min Technicolor saga of a lumberjack's defence of his beloved redwoods, with Wayne Morris and Claire Trevor. The advertisement in the BN Sep 15 1939 included the promise that "All military will be admitted half-price except on Saturdays". The Electric Palace advertisement had no such inducement.

Sun Oct 19 1939

The Lyric opened to the general public for the first time on a Sunday, at 6.45 p.m. for a 7 p.m. start. (The Electric Palace had led the way four weeks before.)

For the first two Sundays the advertisement in the BN could offer only "Programme to be announced". On Nov 12 patrons were treated to two now forgotten films: *Dangerous Fingers* (GB 1937), a romantic crime drama, and *Marines Are Here*.

BN Jun 7 1940

Appearance of the first joint advertisement for the Palace and the Lyric on the takeover of both cinemas by the Dorchester Cinema Company, whose monogram DCC was placed vertically between their names.

From Dec 1 1940 to Apr 27 1941 the same films were frequently shown at both the Palace and the Lyric on a Sunday evening. This became the regular practice from Sept 7 1941 to Apr 26 1942, after which date the Lyric did not open on Sundays – as had already been the case between May 4 and Aug 31 1941.

Sat Sep 27 1947

The Lyric closed "until further notice", its final far from star-studded US double bill being significantly mediocre: *The Notorious Lone Wolf*, with Gerald Mohr as the eponymous gentleman crook, plus *The Return of Rusty*, the tale of a young Czech war orphan (Ted Donaldson) befriended by a boy and his dog (i.e. Rusty).

According to the BN Jan 7 1949 this closure was "owing to film and staff difficulties". On Nov 21 1947 the BN reported that the Dorset County Education Committee were to investigate the possibility of using the Lyric Cinema as a school canteen for the Bridport General Schools. The rent, however, was rather high.

Mon Jan 17 1949

After being thoroughly overhauled and redecorated, the Lyric re-opened with a week-long display of the charms of Linda Darnell in *Forever Amber*, Otto Preminger's bowdlerized Technicolor adaptation of Kathleen Winsor's immensely popular novel about a lively wench at the court of Charles II (played in the film by George Sanders).

BN Aug 17 1962

"Bridport's Lyric Cinema is to close on September 1. This was confirmed by Mr T. McDevitt, manager of the Palace Cinema, speaking to the Bridport News earlier this week. We understand that the closure is due to poor attendances.

At present operated by the Dorchester Cinema Company, the Lyric has been a cinema for over 40 years.

The manager of the Lyric, which seats 200 people, is Mr William Ryan, and his staff of about six will be affected by the decision to close. Said Mr McDevitt, 'we consider that one cinema in the town is sufficient'.

When the 'Electric Palace', as it was known, was first opened, Hollywood was enjoying its golden years as capital of the film world, and talkies were yet to come. Among other things, the building has been used as a Territorial Army Drill Hall, and as a Congregational Chapel.

The premises, owned by trustees on behalf of Liberal interests, incorporate the Liberal Hall, but on special occasions, the Liberal Party reserve the right to hold their meetings in the cinema below.

Closures such as this can often be blamed on the advent of television, and it would seem to have had a severe impact not only on the cinema but on live entertainment, too, in Bridport."

Strictly speaking, it is the hall in Barrack Street that was in use as a cinema for over 40 years – with two interruptions, the first of just over 14 years, the second of just over one year.

On two occasions during the General Election campaign of 1950, on Wed Feb 8 and Wed Feb 22 (eve of poll), the Liberal candidate Grant Cameron held evening meetings in the Lyric.

Sat Sep 1 1962

The Lyric closed, its final programme consisting of: *The Secret Partner* (GB 1961), a 91-min routine thriller starring Stewart Granger; and *Ring of Fire* (US 1961), a 90-min outdoor action movie in Metrocolor, starring David Janssen, with music by guitarist Duane Eddy and a climactic forest conflagration.

The BN reported the closure on Sep 7, informing readers that the cinema premises might be used in future as a hall for various purposes. "The lease, which the [Dorchester] Cinema Company have on the premises, has not yet expired, and negotiations have been taking place between the Company and the trustees."

Since August 1971 the Liberal Hall/Old Artillery Hall/Bridport Electric Palace/ Lyric Cinema/9 Barrack Street has been occupied by Bernard Gale's Bridport School of Dancing.

For details of the films shown at the Lyric, see the history of the (Electric) Palace, South Street, sections 2–4.

After the peak period 1939–46 there was between 1955 and 1965 a decline of 56% in the number of cinemas in the UK, brought about by the growth of television. The following statistics are revealing:

1914	3,170 cinemas in UK	1945	4,723	1962	2,421
1928	3,760	1950	4,584	1963	2,181
1934	4,305	1955	4,483	1965	1,971
1939	4,901	1960	3,034	1975	1,530

In 1920 there were 16 cinematograph halls in Dorset: Blandford, Bovington, Bridport, Chiswell, Dorchester, Easton, Lyme Regis (2), Poole (2), Shaftesbury, Sherborne, Swanage, Weymouth (3).

In 1927 there were still 16 in all, but Lyme Regis had only one, while Parkstone had gained a Victory Palace.

By 1939 the number of cinemas in Dorset had increased to 24: Blandford, Bovington, Bridport (2), Dorchester (2), Easton, Fortuneswell, Gillingham, Lyme Regis (3), Parkstone, Poole (3), Shaftesbury, Sherborne, Swanage, Wareham, Weymouth (3), Wimborne.

At present in Dorset (excluding Bournemouth) there are just 7 full-time cinemas, with a total of 17 screens, namely: The Palace Bridport; The Plaza, Dorchester (2 screens); The Regent, Lyme Regis; UCI Tower Park, Poole (10 screens), The Mowlem, Swanage; The Rex, Wareham; The Picturedrome, Weymouth.

Bridport (Electric) Palace, South Street

I The "Silent" Period: From Monday June 14 1926
to Saturday January 10 1931

Bridport News Feb 17 1922

Extract from the report of the monthly Town Council meeting held on Tue Feb 14 1922:

"Councillor GUPPY, Chairman of the Property Committee, intimated that he had just received a letter from Messrs F. Cooper and Sons, architects, submitting plans for the proposed Cinema and shops in East Street. These, it appeared, had already been approved by the architect of the Dorset County Council and the tenants had also seen them and agreed to the work being proceeded with immediately. To expedite this matter, the architects would be obliged if these plans could be passed, subject to the approval of the Property Committee and complying with the Borough Building Bye-laws. The Company considered that by commencing this work forthwith it would find employment for a number of workmen and help relieve unemployment in the Borough.

Councillor GUPPY remarked that he should have preferred the plans first going before the Property Committee, but in view of the urgency of the work, he would propose that they be passed subject to the approval of the Committee and complying with the Borough Bye-laws.

Councillor DAVEY seconded.

Councillor WEEKS said the Cinema had been talked about for some considerable time and although he was anxious that work should be found for the unemployed he considered it was hardly treating the Council with proper courtesy in springing a large building like this on them without the members having an opportunity of seeing the plans.

Councillor GUPPY: I quite agree with Councillor Weeks. I have not seen the plans myself."

After some discussion the plans were finally passed.

BN Feb 24 1922

"The announcement appearing in last week's issue that Bridport is to have a new Cinema has aroused considerable interest not only among lovers of the 'movies', but the inhabitants generally. We understand that the work will be commenced within a month or six weeks, and every effort will be made to complete the building as soon as possible. In view of the unemployment in the town this new enterprise will be the means of providing considerable work at a most opportune time.

Business premises, opposite the Bull Hotel in East Street, were acquired some months ago by the Company, and it is here that the Cinema is to be erected. The site is an admirable one, in the heart of the town, and there will be ample room, once the task of demolition is complete, of extending the building as far back as Rax Lane.

A Bridport News reporter saw the plan of the proposed building this week, and the ground space will cover a superficial area of about 800 square yards. The Cinema itself will accommodate, roughly, about 550 people, and when complete will be one of the largest and most up-to-date in the county. Comfort and convenience has been studied in detail, and one of the many features of the building will be a balcony from which a splendid view of the films may be obtained. Special attention has also been paid to the provision of exits in case of fire.

The two shops and domestic buildings are to be rebuilt and the whole, when complete, will considerably enhance the appearance of East Street."

BN Jul 14 1922

Extract from the report of the Town Council meeting held on Tue Jul 11:

"Arising out of the report of the Property Committee Councillor WEEKS said that some time ago the Council approved plans for the erection of a cinema in the town. He understood that the work was going to afford immediate work for the unemployed and was to cost about £10,000. He would like to know what had happened since.

Councillor GUPPY (Chairman of the Property Committee): The position is the same now as it was then.

Councillor WEEKS: That is a silly reply!

Councillor GUPPY: Thank you."

A new, specially designed cinema was, of course, never built in East Street, and no further mention of it was made in the BN.

BN Jul 11 1924

Towards the end of the report of the Town Council meeting held on Tue Jul 8 was a brief list of plans passed by the Council, including those for a cinema in South Street for the Bridport Electric Palace Company. These plans, however, underwent such modification that it was necessary to resubmit them nine months later.

Sat Apr 11 1925

Notice of intention by the Bridport Electric Palace Company Limited to build at 35 South Street a new Cinema, Shop, Dressing rooms, Engine room etc. to be used as a Cinema and Theatre was delivered – together with complete plans and a block plan – to the Office of the Borough Surveyor in the late afternoon. Dated April 6th 1925, the document was signed on behalf of the Bridport Electric Palace Co. Ltd by Frederick Cooper and Sons, architects and surveyors (of 6 Victoria Grove), who had drawn up the plans. (Frederick Cooper himself had been Borough Surveyor for more than 40 years, resigning from the post on Jan 13 1925.)

Arriving too late to be considered either by the Property Committee or at the Town Council meeting on Tue Apr 14 1925, the new plans were discussed at the next meeting on Tue May 12. There were problems relating to the western portion of the cinema, which would be brought near to the dwelling house of Mr Hider to within seven feet of his living room window. It was consequently agreed to refer the plans back to the Property Committee.

Such problems were eventually overcome, and amended plans were approved on Tue Jun 9 1925.

The rather unusual site, set back from the road, was previously occupied by the coal yard of Leonard Stembridge, wholesale and retail fruit and fish merchant, coal merchant and shipping agent.

The Bridport Museum has copies of the architects' plans of the building.

Sat May 29 1926

The Palace in Barrack Street closed, after providing Bridport with a pleasing variety of film entertainment for 14¼ years.

Announcement of Grand Opening Performance on Monday, June 14th at the New Electric Palace, South Street – managing director: Sydney C. Shepherd.

Elsewhere in the newspaper the new building was described in some detail:

"Monday, June 14th is the opening date of Bridport's new picture theatre. It will mark another milestone in the van of progress in which this little town of ours is taking so prominent a part, and moreover it will provide those who seek relaxation and pleasure with a building handsome in appearance and admirable in design.

The whole of the interior has been carried out with extreme care and thoroughness, and as a result from the time the patron steps inside the entrance hall he will perceive no discordant lines in the whole composition of the building and its prevailing tone of decoration.

It will be entered from South Street through a covered archway and glazed entrance. The theatre itself is set back about 50 feet from the street and facing it are the main entrance doors with pay-box centrally situated, and accommodation for cycles on the right. On the opposite side there is a glazed passage providing a separate entrance to the front seats, and also emergency exits through Mr Tucker's yard into Folly Lane. On this passage cloak-rooms are provided for both ladies and gentlemen.

On entering the main building from the front on the ground floor is the foyer or entrance hall, which is spacious and well lighted, measuring 23 ft by 22 ft and about 16 ft in height, and paved with Terrazzo. To the left of the foyer there is a wide staircase leading to the circle, also paved in Terrazzo, while on the right are well arranged cloakrooms of ample size for ladies and gentlemen, together with private storerooms, etc.

The auditorium is entered by two doors off the foyer, and is a hall 64 ft in length by 38 ft wide, and about 27 ft high. It is planned and designed on the very latest style with properly raked floor and curved ceiling. The interior is Georgian with cornices, panels and moulded ceiling ribs in fibrous plaster – the colour and general scheme being most appropriate. The seating accommodation on the ground floor is sufficient for about 400 people.

Off the main stairs leading to the circle is the manager's office, replete in every detail. On the first floor there is a large lounge measuring 38 ft by 14 ft by 10 ft 6 ins in height. This is also Terrazzo paved. Situate away from the lounge are cloakrooms for ladies and gentlemen.

The circle is entered by three doors from the lounge. In the circle provision has been made for six tiers of seats, and at the rear will be found two boxes, providing in all accommodation for about 100 patrons.

Facing the foyer at the east end of the auditorium is the proscenium opening to the stage 32 ft wide by 21 ft high. In front of this is the orchestra well. Inside the proscenium opening is the stage running the full width of the auditorium and measuring 38 ft by 20 ft. Behind the stage are the dressing rooms, green room, loading dock, artistes entrance, corridors and engine room, whilst in the basement under the stage are arranged retiring rooms and stores, and under the green room is the heating chamber.

Every care has been taken by the Company in providing a building of the latest description both as regards planning, design and equipment. The comfort of patrons has been studied in every detail, heating, lighting, and ventilation being all taken into consideration, as well as safety from fire. The building has been constructed of fire resisting materials, and there is also ample provision of appliances with which to deal with any possible outbreak.

The screen and machines are of the latest improved type, and affixed in the projection chamber are fire shutters that can be instantly released. One of the principal features of the building is the level front projection which ensures an absence of distortion from any seat. The first row of seats will be 30 ft from the screen, and every seat has a perfect and unobstructed view of the screen and stage.

The management is placed in the capable hands of Mr Sidney Shepherd, and with such an experienced person at the helm the future success of the Cinema would seem assured. The Company have under consideration extensive alterations to the adjoining properties in the front facing South Street, but for the present these will be deferred until a later date.

The heating and ventilation scheme has been carefully considered and this work has been carried out by Messrs G. N. Haden and Sons, Ltd, of Trowbridge. The electric lighting plant has been provided through Mr H. N. Harris, of Bridport, who, in conjunction with Messrs Stanley Cooper and Co. Ltd, of Bournemouth, have carried out all the wiring, lighting, fittings and other electrical equipment. The gas for power and pilot lighting is supplied by the Bridport Gas Co.

The architects are Messrs Frederick Cooper and Sons, of Bridport, and the builders and general contractors Messrs Jesty and Baker, of Weymouth, whose foreman, Mr J. Harvey has been in charge of the work.

The other subcontractors are: Constructional steelwork, Gardiner Sons and Co. Ltd, Bristol; Terrazzo paving, Marble Mosaic Co. Ltd, Charles Street, Bristol; fibrous plaster, Messrs H. E. Gaze, Ltd, Euston Road, London; seating etc., Messrs Geo. Pixton and Co. Ltd, Soho Square, London; cinematograph and stage equipment, Messrs Walturdaws Ltd, Gerrard Street, London; carpets etc., Messrs Northover and Gilbert, Bridport."

The BN Jun 11 1926 revealed that the piano, a Steinway, was supplied by Messrs Duck, Son and Pinker, of Bath, through Mr Hawkins, their local agent.

Mon Jun 14 1926

The New Electric Palace was opened by the Mayor, Mr F. Weeks, accompanied on the stage by Major J. A. Atherton, Mr Shepherd and the Mayoress, who was presented after the opening with a bouquet by the manager's little niece, Miss Janet Knight.

The Mayor's speech was reported in the BN Jun 18. Its nature and tone may be judged by the following two extracts:

"He hoped the directors would not regard the undertaking as being complete until there was an improvement to the street frontage. Then, he was sure, they would have a cinema equal to any in this part of the country –(applause)– and would provide further evidence that Bridport was not lagging behind any other place, even in the matter of cinemas, electric light, or an up-to-date fire brigade (applause)."

"He noticed from a publication called 'Pictureland' that the proprietors intended to cater for all classes, and he hoped they would see more British pictures of an educational character rather than some of the sensational American films (applause)."

What he and the rest of the packed audience saw at that first evening performance, due to start at 7.30, was in fact Franco-American, a special attraction: Gloria Swanson in *Madame Sans-Gêne*. From Laundress to Duchess, from Napoleon's Wash-Lady to the Emperor's Court. For over 30 years an International Stage Success, now a Screen Classic. This 110 min adaptation of the Comédie Française 1893 hit comedy by Sardou and Marceau was directed for Paramount by Léonce Perret and made on location in France, using locales associated with the Napoleonic period.

It is instructive to compare this sophisticated opening programme with the six one-reelers shown at the Electric Palace in Barrack Street on its first evening just over 14 years previously.

"The projection of the pictures was excellent. They were clear, flickerless, and perfect in focus, and the whole programme was thoroughly enjoyed. The machines were operated on this occasion under the supervision of Mr Ivor E. Faull, of the Walturdaw Cinema Company."

Patrons had paid 6d, 1/- or 1/6 for their stall seats, and 2/- for the balcony. Children under 12 paid the full price on opening night, but thereafter got in half-price when accompanied by an adult, except on Saturday nights.

The BN June 18 1926 commented also in its Weekly Notes column on this important occasion:

"The management of Bridport's new Electric Picture Palace have every cause for self-congratulation on their venture. Monday was 'opening night' and the townspeople gave their support solidly to the new enterprise so much so, that although the building can accommodate 500, a great many had to be refused admission, but it could not be helped. These good people, however, have since given their patronage and can almost be looked upon as regular patrons now. Everyone spoke in praise of the beautiful interior of the building and the wonderful clarity in which the pictures were shown.

For many months passed (sic) work had been proceeding steadily with the erection of the building. When the frontage has been completed, then from the point of view of entrance and from the internal aspect, Bridport's new picture palace will compare very favourably with similar places of entertainment in the Provinces. One who has done much hard work, 'behind the scenes' as it were, has been Mr J. C. Palmer, the Chairman of the Directors, who has been very assiduous in supervising the work and attending to the many details appertaining to the creation of so large a building for public use."

Mr Palmer had earlier in the evening of Jun 14 entertained the Mayor, friends, the cinema's architects, builders etc. to dinner at the Greyhound Hotel. Apparently he was keen to provide Bridport with a theatre for operatic performances, but realised that only a combined cinema and theatre would be economically viable.

After opening night, performances were continuous from 6 to 10 Monday to Saturday, with matinees announced for 2.30 every Wednesday and Saturday, but these were almost immediately cancelled and did not fully resume until the beginning of 1927.

In that first week *Madame Sans-Gêne* was shown on Tuesday and Wednesday. On Thursday the programme changed to *Sally of the Sawdust* (US 1925), a 104-min realistic circus story, directed by D. W. Griffith and starring W. C. Fields. The practice of changing the programme each Monday and Thursday had been normal at the Barrack Street Palace and continued at the new South Street cinema, though some films were considered to be so important and/or popular that they were booked for a week.

BN Aug 6 1926

The advertisement is now headed The Electric Palace, the initial epithet "New" having been dropped.

BN Aug 27 1926

The advertisement included two photographs of the auditorium. These were reproduced nine years later as part of the Electric Palace's full-page general advertisement on page 1 of the second (1935) edition of *The Port Bredy of Wessex – Some Account of the History and Charms of BRIDPORT and its surroundings*, edited by Alderman E. S. Reynolds, J.P. and published by the Borough Council.

BN Sep 24 1926

"ACTOR RETURNS HOME TO WITNESS FILM AT BRIDPORT

More than usual interest centred round the film *The Little French Girl*, which has been shown at the Electric Palace during the early part of this week on account of the fact that Mr Anthony Jowitt of Strode Manor was acting in the role of Capt. Owen.

Curiously enough Mr Jowitt was in the neighbourhood at the time and took the opportunity of witnessing the picture for the first time since its completion. Interviewed by a representative of the 'Bridport News' he expressed great admiration for the theatre which he found most comfortable and surprisingly large.

Mr Anthony Jowitt is the eldest son of Mr and Mrs E. M. Jowitt of Strode Manor near here. *The Little French Girl* was his first experience of motion picture acting. He went to America with the intention of writing but on meeting Jesse Lasky the vice-president of the Famous Players–Lasky Corp. the latter decided that Mr Jowitt has possibilities as an actor and signed him to a contract. Mr Jowitt was glad to accept the contract as it afforded him unrivalled opportunities of seeing the methods in vogue at the studios and so was of great benefit to him as a writer of stories for the screen.

He intends to spend about two or three months in England and on his return to the United States will concentrate on the directing and writing end of the picture business."

He was seen again on the Bridport screen in early December, sharing the billing with Gloria Swanson (who played three parts) in *The Coast of Folly* – converted in the BN advertisement into The Cost of Folly.

The Little French Girl was a romantic drama, "filmed on a sumptuous scale" and adapted from "the sensational novel of French morals and manners by Anne Douglas Sedgwick", its central theme: should a daughter suffer for the indiscretions of her mother? The main role was taken by the charming 17-year-old Mary Brian, who had made her film debut as Wendy in *Peter Pan* in 1924. Jowitt was 22.

The Little French Girl was directed by Irish-born Herbert Brenon, one of the most important Hollywood directors of the 1920s. He had directed *Peter Pan* and later made the first and highly successful film of P. C. Wren's bestseller "Beau Geste", starring Ronald Colman and Mary Brian and shown to Bridport audiences in March 1928.

Jowitt was sufficiently active and important to appear in the biographical section of artistes in the first edition of The Picturegoer's Who's Who and Encyclopaedia of the Screen Today, published by Odhams Press in 1933. However, he is not included in Halliwell's Filmgoer's Companion or Ephraim Katz's International Film Encyclopedia.

Mon Sep 27 to Sat Oct 2 1926

The first film to be shown all week: *The Merry Widow*, directed by Erich von Stroheim and starring Mae Murray and John Gilbert.

Lehar's music was available to the cinema pianist, backed up by the "special engagement of Millicent Burton and Stanley Rose, Continental speciality dancers, to dance The Merry Widow Waltz Prologue at each performance throughout the week, as performed by them at all the leading supercinemas in the country".

Some patrons perhaps were in a position to compare the cinema experience with the George Edwardes Daly's Theatre production of this musical comedy at the Pavilion Theatre Weymouth on Sep 17 and 18.

Thu Oct 21 to Sat Oct 23 1926

Showing of the first episode of the serial *The Radio Detective*, a screen version in ten parts of Arthur B. Reeve's latest novel.

By arrangement with Mr Shepherd the Bridport News had secured the serial rights to the novel and the first of 15 instalments had appeared in the Oct 1 issue. Announcing this coup, the BN Sep 24 had strongly advised all its readers to follow the adventures of the Radio Detective in its columns, and afterwards see the picture. Further encouragement had been given in the BN Oct 8: "Active, healthy minds crave adventure and mystery. Our new serial story by Mr A. B. Reeve is clean, wholesome, educational and inspiring. The plot is absorbing in interest, and each chapter teems with action. Fascinating threads of scientific information are interwoven with painstaking care to form an entertaining, brilliant narrative ... All wireless enthusiasts and Boy Scouts will await the first episode of the picture with pleasurable anticipation."

The detective hero was Craig Kennedy, a scientific investigator created by the American mystery writer A. B. Reeve (1880–1936) and featured in a series of eleven novels between 1916 and 1925. An earlier series of stories by Reeve had become the basis for three of Pearl White's most successful serials, *The Exploits of Elaine*, *The New Exploits of Elaine* and *The Romance of Elaine*, all made in 1915.

In 1956 the story of *Cockleshell Heroes* was serialized in the BN some weeks before the film reached the Palace.

Three film serials, all in ten parts, were shown in 1927: *Strings of Steel*, about the pioneer telephone engineers who "blazed the trail of steel through the air more than 50 years ago"; *The Green Archer*, from Edgar Wallace's thriller; and *The Flame Fighter*, a story of the thrilling life of the firemen, with the English-born Hollywood silent star Herbert Rawlinson. Thereafter, however, the serial was no longer a regular item in the programme. Several series continued to be shown, e.g. *London After Dark*, *On With the Dance*, *Pathé Song Cartunes*, *Everyday Frauds*, *Eve's Review*.

Thu Oct 28 1926

Bridport Carnival day in aid of the Hospital and District Nursing Society. The event was marred by rain, which fortunately stopped just before the start of the Torchlight Procession at 6 p.m. That evening, to avoid a clash with this highlight of the carnival, there was only one performance at the Electric Palace (commencing at 7.45) of *With Cobham to the Cape*, "a record of a Modern Adventurer and detailed incidents of his 17,000 Miles Flight. A Picture everybody should see". (Alan Cobham, accompanied by engineer Arthur Elliott and Gaumont photographer B. W. G. Emmott, had set off in a DH50J biplane from London on Nov 16 1925 to survey an air route to South Africa for Imperial Airways, arriving back at Croydon on Mar 13 1926.)

But there was live entertainment, too, at the Electric Palace. "It was a happy suggestion on the part of Mr G. Hann that the Bridport Revue party should give a performance in the Town Hall at the close of the carnival, for the building was crowded with an appreciative audience. Under the direction of Miss Hallett the party quite excelled themselves. The singing was bright and vivacious and so pleased were the members of the audience with the programme provided that many visited the Electric Palace later in the night when the same party gave another equally enjoyable concert" (BN Nov 5 1926).

This second show at the cinema raised £3 6s 6d.

Mon Nov 29 to Sat Dec 4 1926

For the first time Mr Shepherd engaged – at great expense – a variety turn to augment the film programme: Bryant and Betty, direct from the Principal London and Provincial Halls with their Australian novelty act and Original Electric Juggling Scena. Artistically Staged and Dressed.

The following week the special six-day attraction on stage, personally presented by Dr Edward Morehen, was the Amazing Hooded Woman (The White Witch Doctor), direct from her practice of Mystic Rites in Central Africa. She will gladly solve your life's problems. Just write your question on paper, initial it, and keep it. Her answer will astonish and please you.

There was a special matinee for ladies only on Wednesday at 2.30 p.m., with seats at 2/-, 1/6 and 1/-. "No Pictures will be shown, and no Gentlemen or Children will be admitted."

Dr Morehen returned the following year – see Dec 12–17 1927.

Other live entertainers brought in during this period to augment the film programme include

For a week:
1927   The Carryls Trio, comprising two ladies and one gent in a delightful musical and dancing act that is quite out of the ordinary (Jan)

The Musical Dawsons – one Lady and one Gent playing eight different instruments (Jan/Feb)

Jack Revel and Dorothy Hall – "The Modern Entertainers" in Original Comedy and Grand Opera (May)

Basil King, the Ventriloquial "Monarch" (direct from Maskelyne's Theatre, London) presenting his Company of Talking Figures in the Novel Sketch "The Inspector and the Policeman" (May)

1928   Henry Bekker – the Famous Magical Humourist in Tricks and Talk (Mar)

Jeavon and Jena in a pleasing equilibristic sensational novelty (Apr/May)

The Regina Floria Trio (Ladies), in remarkable feats of strength on Rings, Rope and Trapeze (Jul). The films that week, rather appropriately, were *The Woman Who Didn't Care*, starring ex-model and Ziegfeld girl Lilyan Tashman, and *What Happened to Father?* with Warner Oland.

For three days:
1927   The Bridport Revue Chorus, in a special new programme (Mar)

1930 The Brix Sisters, in a Clever Burlesque, Singing and Illusion Act (Feb)
      The celebrated musical Arco, Danzette Trio, with Novel Instruments, Beautiful
      Dancing and Clever Comedy. Do not miss hearing ARCO and his Wonderful
      Piano Accordion (Mar)
      Paulin Haslock, the Famous Mystic and Escapologist in Mystery and Thrills
      (Dec)

For one evening only:
1927 Miss Margery Whetham's pupils in exhibition dances (Fri Apr 22)
      Miss Effie Northover's pupils in a short cabaret show (Fri Apr 29)
1928 Miss Effie Northover's pupils from Weymouth gave a short cabaret show
      (Mon Jan 16). The main film on this evening was *The Flag Lieutenant*,
      starring Henry Edwards, "mostly produced on H.M.S. Tiger at Weymouth, and
      exactly as presented at a Royal Performance before the KING and QUEEN and
      PRINCESS MARY". The film received a second presentation in Bridport a
      fortnight later, Feb 2–4.

Mon Dec 13 1926

As was the practice at the Palace in Barrack Street from 1923, Grand Benefit
Performance in aid of the Mayor's Christmas Fund. In addition to the film programme
– the main attraction being the comedy *What Happened to Jones* (US 1926), starring
the popular English actor Reginald Denny in "one of the funniest and most farcical
pictures he has made" – there were songs by the Hutchings' Symondsbury Quartette,
dances by Miss Dulcie Gibbs, choruses by the Revue Troupe and music by Stoodley's
Syncopated Seven with the latest London successes. The cinema was crowded, and
during an interval the Mayor (Mr A. R. Travers), after expressing his gratitude to the
Palace directors and the performers, briefly explained the origin and administration of
the fund and concluded by thanking the audience for coming there that night and
enabling him to distribute happiness and joy into the lives of their fellow men this
yuletide.

These pre-Christmas benefit performances were to continue until the outbreak of
the Second World War.

Mon Jan 24 to Wed Jan 26 1927

The first pantomime on the Electric Palace Stage: The Forty Thieves – three evening
performances and a Wed matinee – presented by comedian Wilfrid Dane, an all-star
cast of over 30 artistes and a full London chorus.

The report in the BN Jan 28 was most encouraging. "The success that has
attended the pantomime 'The Forty Thieves', staged at the Electric Palace in the early
part of this week by Mr Wilfrid Dane, should prove an incentive to the management to
provide further diversions of this kind.

On Monday evening it is doubtful whether there was a happier man in Bridport
than Mr Dane. As he said at the conclusion of the first night performance, he was very
gratified by the appreciation shown and the patronage given. Bridport people will
remember when he ran a show one summer at West Bay, and it had not been a success.
He had said then that, when Bridport had a hall sufficiently large, he would bring a
pantomime which they would appreciate; and they would all agree that he had

achieved his object. 'The Forty Thieves' was enjoyed by all who saw it – and there were packed audiences every night."

Further diversions of this kind were provided each year, indeed in 1928 Bridport was treated to two pantomimes: Wilfrid Dane's "Mother Goose" in January, Carlton Fredrick's "Jack and the Beanstalk" (libretto and lyrics by Wilfrid Dane) in early February. In 1930 W. Ellis Slack's "Beauty and the Beast" was retained for the rest of the week owing to its Enormous Success, thus ousting *His Destiny*, "a magnificent film produced mostly on the Prince of Wales' Ranch in Canada".

Tue Mar 1 1927

The Bridport Amateur Dramatic Society presented the popular play "Lord Richard in the Pantry" on stage, with selections of music given by the Bohemian Blues Orchestra during the evening. Tickets were somewhat more expensive than for the usual screen entertainment, being 3/6, 2/4, 1/6 and 9d; the proceeds went to the Bridport Hospital. A further performance of the play took place in the Electric Palace on Fri Jul 22 (see also Aug 10–12 1931).

On Tue Dec 20 the BADS put on Frederick Lonsdale's "The Last of Mrs Cheyney", the first amateur production of this play in the country. Incidental music between the acts was provided by Mr E. Draper and his orchestra. Ticket prices ranged from 4/9 to 1/-, the beneficiary this time being the Bridport Cricket, Lawn Tennis and Bowls Club.

The first film version of Lonsdale's 1925 comedy-thriller, with Norma Shearer and Basil Rathbone in the main roles, was shown at the Palace in Aug 1930 in a silent print, returning in Mar 1933 with audible dialogue.

Touring companies were booked during this period to present plays on the stage in the first half of the week:

Mar 5–7 1928 George M. Cohan's "Broadway Jones" – a scream in four acts, starring Harry Piddock, produced by Seymour Hicks.

Sep 17–19 1928 The Apollo Theatre, London, production of "The Man Who Changed His Name", a new comedy thriller by Edgar Wallace.

Aug 18–20 1930 A First-Class West-End Company in the farce "He Walked in Her Sleep", direct from a run at the London Vaudeville.

The seat prices in 1928 were 3/-, 2/4, 1/10, 1/2; by 1930 these had dropped to 2/4, 1/10, 1/6, 1/-.

BN Jul 15 1927

"Mr Shepherd informs us that he has made arrangements for a cinematograph cameraman to come from London to take a film of tomorrow's Hospital Carnival. He hopes to be able to take each entry separately in West Allington before the procession starts, then scenes in the town during its progress. Given fine weather the merry crowds should make a good picture. Tuesday next is the earliest day on which the picture can be shown, and it will be included at each performance for the remainder of the week."

Mon Sep 26 to Sat Oct 1 1927

Showing of the film of the Immortal Retreat from *Mons*, directed by Captain Walter Summers, one of a series of reconstructions of Great War battles made for British Instructional Films. It was presented at all performances with full effects, and a well-received song prologue was given each evening by Mr Joe Reed, who in Mar 1929 rendered a similar service to the fifth film version of *Uncle Tom's Cabin* (with its cast of over 5,000 and cost of some £400,000).

On Wed Sep 28 there was a Special Military Night under the distinguished patronage of Lieut.-Col. Sir John V. E. Lees, Bart., DSO, MC, Commanding Officer of the 4th Battalion Dorset Regiment. Members of the 4th Battalion and the 224th Dorset Battery were present as guests of the management. "Prior to the screening of the film Mr J. Reed roused the martial spirit of the audience by his fine rendering of 'The Deathless Army'. Possessing a rich baritone voice, Mr Reed really excelled himself on this occasion and there was a spontaneous outburst of applause from all parts of the house" (BN Sep 39 1927).

The first film of this series of Great War battle reconstructions – an account of the Battle of Jutland – had been shown in Barrack Street in Feb 1922. It is interesting to note in this context that in Dec 1929 Palace patrons could see *When Fleet Meets Fleet*, a romantic drama centring on a pre-war friendship between a British and a German Naval Commander, who are both in love with the same girl and then find themselves on opposite sides in the Battle of Jutland. Earl Jellicoe, who was in command of the Grand Fleet on May 31 1916, praised the film for its faithful portrayal of the engagement and for its treatment of the conflict between love and devotion to duty.

On Thu Oct 6 1927 *The Jazz Singer*, the first (part-) talkie to be widely seen, was given its première at Warners' Theatre on Broadway, followed by that of the first 100% all-talking movie, *Lights of New York*, on Jul 6 1928 at the Strand Theater, New York. The talkies had arrived, but were not to reach Bridport for some time.

Mon Oct 31 to Wed Nov 2 1927

Replacing the film programme were Les Vivandieres, a concert party in a novelty cabaret show, under the direction of and including the comedienne Della Fredricks. Tickets: 2/4, 2/-, 1/6, 1/2 – children full price. The show was so popular that the manager brought Les Vivandieres back the following year (Oct 22–24 1928).

Other stage entertainments of this type, providing a live alternative to films, were

For three days:
1928   W. Ellis Slack's Cabaret Follies of 1928 – a Revue of Bits and Pieces, including the famous Hot Steppers Band conducted by Professor Popoffski (Jun)
    The XL's concert party – a Production of Mirth and Merriment under the direction of and including Wilfrid Dane, the West Country's Favourite (Jul/Aug)
1929   The famous Piccadilly Follies, a lively cabaret revue on a special flying visit (Jan/Feb)
1930   Showfolk – first announced as Snowfolk – the Last Word in modern cabaret entertainment (May)
    Hot Punch – a Quick-Fire Show of all that is best in vaudeville (Sep)

For one evening:

Mon Feb 20 1928 The Dorchester Follies, who were back with Mirth, Music and Mimicry on Fri Apr 5 1929 – on both occasions in aid of the Marshwood School Building Fund.

Wed Apr 25 1928 At 7.45 Miss Effie Northover and Miss Norah Medcalf, MAM, presented a children's Dancing and Dramatic Display of 50 performers. The programme included a Chinese legend "The Singing Soul", a Woodland Fantasy ballet, several dance scenas (The Half Holiday, Les Amours de Columbine etc.), "The Pied Piper of Hamelin" in mime and costume, operatic and character solo and group dances, recitations and songs. Ticket prices were quite high, ranging from 3/6 to 1/2, and attendance that evening was only fair. "Each youthful artiste acquitted herself nobly, and it seemed a great pity that such a praiseworthy performance did not attract a much larger audience" (BN Apr 27 1928) – regrets not unknown to the present-day Arts Centre management.

This display replaced Constance Talmadge in a sparkling French farce *Breakfast at Sunrise*, which could, however, be seen during the afternoon at a 2.30 matinee.

Mon Dec 12 to Sat Dec 17 1927

Dr Edward Morehen (in Person) presented on the stage his Golden Cloak – a Prophetic Mystery of the Ancients. The Traditional Wisdom of 2,000 Years with the Experience of the Modern Scientist. There was a special matinee for ladies only (over the age of 16), but without the film programme; the seat prices for this were 2/-, 1/6 with a limited number at 1/-.

The bare facts of the advertisement, which carried a photograph of the mysterious Doctor, were given a little more substance by an article on the same page of the BN Dec 9 1927, illustrated by a different photographic portrait. It ran as follows:

"Dr Edward Morehen will present what he terms the World's Oldest Mystery in conjunction with his Golden Cloak. Having lived amongst, and studied the way of, the Maoris, Indians and Orientals who make witchcraft a feature of their daily lives, he developed a faculty which is little short of supernatural and comes prepared to freely use this mysterious knowledge for the benefit of his own race.

Dr Morehen puts this gift to practical utility by solving any problem of doubt you may have concerning your own affairs. All you are asked to do is to concentrate your mind upon whatever you want to know by writing it down on a piece of paper, initialling it and keeping it in your pocket. The answers are always interesting, sometimes instructive and often screamingly funny.

As it must be perfectly obvious that all questions cannot be dealt with in the presence of a mixed audience, Dr Morehen will hold a special seance matinee for ladies only on Wednesday at 2.30. All ladies are cordially invited, for this demonstration is totally unlike those given in the evenings."

The films following Dr Morehen's performance were: Mon–Wed *The Road to Mandalay*, starring Lon Chaney as Singapore Joe, an evil saloon-keeper with a cataract in one eye, and Thu–Sat *The Lure of the Wild* with Jane Novak and "Lightning", a Wonderful Dog.

Thu Dec 22 1927

For the Benefit Night in aid of the Mayor's Christmas Fund the main film was *The Exquisite Sinner*, a comedy-drama starring Renée Adorée, best known for her performance in *The Big Parade*, which had been shown at the Electric Palace in mid-October. Miss Margery Whetham's pupils gave a dancing display, and there were vocal items from the Bridport Revue Girls.

Mon Jan 9 to Sat Jan 14 1928

Secured at enormous expense, the World's Greatest Film Triumph, *Ben Hur*, starring Ramon Novarro, Francis X. Bushman and May McAvoy, nightly at 6 and 8.20 (separate houses), with matinees at 2.15 on Wed, Thu and Sat, and a special matinee for children on Saturday morning at 10.15. All seats were reserved and prices increased to 2/4, 2/-, 1/3 and 9d – children full price at all performances except the morning matinee.

The advertisement in the BN Jan 6 1928 was extra large and abnormally headed "The Palace, Bridport". The newspaper gave further details of the film's production and success, how it had taken three years to make at a cost of £1 million. "And, never before has a film attracted so many notables. The Prince of Wales, the King and Queen of the Belgians, the Queens of Spain and Norway, the Princess Royal, Princess Marie Louise, Princess Victoria and Princess Beatrice, are but a few of the Royalty who witnessed 'Ben Hur' there [i.e. at the Tivoli, London], prior to the command performance at Windsor."

It would appear that comments were made about the copy of the film projected at the Electric Palace, with the result that the manager felt it necessary to write to the BN.

"Dear Sir, – My attention has been drawn to a rumour circulating in the town to the effect that the film of 'Ben Hur' which I presented last week had been greatly reduced from that shown in London, and that several scenes had been taken out. I should therefore be obliged if you would kindly insert a copy of the enclosed letter which shows this rumour to be without foundation. Thanking you in anticipation for inserting this letter.

Yours faithfully,
SYDNEY C. SHEPHERD
Manager, Electric Palace, Bridport

January 18th, 1928

COPY

S. C. Shepherd Esq.,
The Electric Palace,
Bridport, Dorset.

1st December, 1927

Dear Sir, – In reply to your letter of the 30th November re 'Ben Hur' you may rest assured that the copy which will be sent to you on January 9th next will be exactly the same production as was shown at the Tivoli, London, with such phenomenal success for 49 weeks, and that no alteration whatsoever will be made. The length is 11,400 feet. Wishing you every success with the film.

Yours faithfully,
JURY-METRO-GOLDWYN, LTD,
W. G. S. LEGER MONTAGUE"

So Bridport audiences did see every minute of this 2¼-hour epic with its spectacular naval battle and chariot race – and nearly 35 years later, during the week Nov 26–Dec 1 1962, the Palace presented the 1959 3½-hour Technicolor remake, with Charlton Heston, Stephen Boyd and Haya Harareet.

Tue May 1 1928

Death of Mr J. C. Palmer at the age of 73. As the BN May 4 noted: "His business activities included a controlling interest in the Electric Palace, a palatial building that ranks as one of the finest in Dorset".

Throughout the week flags were flown at half-mast at the Town Hall, the Conservative Club and the Picture Palace. Mr Shepherd attended the funeral on Fri May 4; among the many floral tokens of sympathy was one from the Manager and Staff of the Bridport Electric Palace as well as one from the Members and Officers of the Bridport Electric Palace Co., Ltd.

Thu Jun 7 and Fri Jun 8 1928

The Symondsbury Village Drama Society presented "Iolanthe" on the stage, with the proceeds going to the Parish Church Restoration Fund. On Saturday Warner Bros' popular German shepherd Rin-Tin-Tin provided the main entertainment with *Tracked by the Police.*

BN Aug 3 1928

"'Would you recognise your favourite screen player if he or she wore a mask?' This is the question that has appeared on all the 'Palace' advertisements for the last week or so, and has aroused a great amount of interest. Patrons will have an opportunity of answering this question, and also of winning one of the prizes amounting to £325 which are being offered by the 'Weekly Dispatch' in the 'Masked Players Contest' during the next five weeks.

The competition comprises a series of five films, each containing a number of well-known film stars, masked or otherwise disguised, and the audience is asked by means of clues given to name the players. The first film is being shown during this week-end, and the remaining four will be shown the last half of each week following. The 'Weekly Dispatch' gives further particulars and the necessary coupon for entering this interesting competition."

MGM were the filmmakers – the "Weekly Dispatch" was a Sunday newspaper. The final unmasked film of the Masked Players Contest was shown from Thu Sep 27 to Sat Sep 29 1928.

Mon Nov 19 to Sat Nov 24 1928

The world-famous O'Mara Opera Company presented seven operas: The Tales of Hoffmann, Faust, Carmen, W. V. Wallace's Maritana, Il Trovatore, Balfe's The Bohemian Girl and The Barber of Seville. Ticket prices were the same as those for the annual pantomimes: 3/6, 2/4, 1/10 and 1/2.

This touring company, founded in 1912 by the distinguished Irish tenor Joseph O'Mara (1861–1927), had been performing at the Pavilion, Weymouth, in the first week of October with a similar programme of seven operas (no Rossini, instead Donizetti's The Daughter of the Regiment).

The BN Nov 9 1928 commented on the forthcoming musical treat: "The week commencing November 19th should set the seal as to whether Bridport wants opera or not. Mr Shepherd writes: 'I believe that never before has an Opera Company of this magnitude appeared in Bridport, and I have booked it feeling convinced that there arc sufficient opera lovers here to make it at least a "meeting expenses proposition".'"

It would appear from the report in the BN Nov 23 1928 that the manager may have been over-optimistic. "The famous O'Mara Opera Company, whose engagement is drawing to a close, have been enthusiastically received at each performance. The size of the audience on the first two nights was not what an attraction of this merit deserved but what they lacked in numbers was made up for in expressions of appreciation and congratulations to Mr Shepherd for bringing to Bridport an entertainment that is seldom seen outside much larger towns than this."

A silent film version of *The Bohemian Girl*, first shown at the Palace, Barrack Street, in Jan 1924, had reappeared at the Electric Palace Sep 13–15 1926 and during its run Mrs T. Thear had sung several of the well-known songs from the opera. The film had an outstanding cast, including Ivor Novello, Gladys Cooper, Constance Collier, C. Aubrey Smith and Ellen Terry, but could no doubt not compete with a fully live performance.

Thu Nov 29 to Sat Dec 1 1928

Showing of *Annie Laurie*, a thrilling story of bonnie Scotland at the time of the Glencoe Massacre, starring Lillian Gish. It was preceded on stage each evening by a Dance Prologue given by the pupils of Miss Margery Whetham and Miss Dulcie Gibbs and consisting of the Highland Fling and a Sword Dance. The film itself – not one of MGM's or Gish's best – has been described as a soggy haggis.

Mon Dec 10 1928

The annual Benefit Night for the Mayor's Christmas Fund – the main films being *The Bugle Call*, starring 13-year-old Jackie Coogan, and *A Half Pint Hero*, with acrobatic comic Lupino Lane. "Both performances were largely attended, and in addition to an excellent programme of pictures, songs were rendered by Mr J. Reed and Mrs E. G. Cuff, dances were given by the pupils of Miss Dulcie Gibbs and Miss Effie Northover; and selections by Bridport Artillery Band, conducted by Mr E. J. Rees, RMSM. Every item was enthusiastically received .... The spendid sum of £16 14s 4d was realised, this being over £4 in excess of last year's effort" (BN Dec 14 1928).

BN Jan 4 1929

First appearance of the advertising slogan describing the Electric Palace as "the cosiest little theatre in the county". It was used for the last time in the advertisement in the BN Mar 6 1931.

Thu Feb 7 to Sat Feb 9 1929

The first production of the Bridport Amateur Operatic Society: "The Mikado" – three evening performances starting at 8 and a Saturday matinee, with ticket prices ranging from 4/9 to 1/2. The BAOS advertisement helpfully advised Beaminster Gilbert and Sullivan lovers that there was a late bus to get them home on Saturday evening.

The orchestra was conducted by Mr E. J. Rees, who was in the cinema again later in the month (Feb 25–27) conducting the Bridport Artillery Band in a Special Musical

Interlude – the main film in the programme being *The House of Deceit*, with Barbara Bedford and Robert Ellis, an unusual drama of modern life centring round a young widow and her son.

The sequence of annual BAOS productions continued until the outbreak of the Second World War – three evenings and a matinee, usually in February (1930, 1931, 1933, 1937–39), sometimes in April (1932, 1934, 1936) and once in May (1935). The first post-war production was in April 1947 in Church House with the run extended to six evenings and a Saturday matinee.

Mon Feb 18 to Wed Feb 20 1929

Showing of the film of Anita Loos' best-known 1925 novel (one of Churchill's favourite books), the hilarious *Gentlemen Prefer Blondes*, starring Ruth Taylor and Clara Bow's closest rival, Alice White. The musicalized and updated 1953 version with Jane Russell and Marilyn Monroe was shown at the Lyric for three days in Dec 1955.

From Mar 15 1929 the BN advertisement informed patrons that "Special Late 'Buses leave after the last performance every Saturday Night for Burton Bradstock, West Bay, Chideock and Morcombelake". This information appeared for the rest of 1929 and throughout 1930.

Mon Jun 17 to Sat Jun 22 1929

The film programme was supplemented by Mr E. Richard and his famous film and stage Alsation dog actor, Robert of St John, together with Miss Gertrude Ford (soprano), direct from the Palladium, London.

"'Bob' as he is known is not of the usual trick variety, but demonstrates on the stage the usefulness of a dog in protecting his master's life and property, which has endeared him to every audience wherever he has appeared. One of his many feats is to release his master from a gag and ropes, a trick which has not been performed by any other dog. No dog lover should miss this canine wonder who may justly be described to be England's Rin-Tin-Tin" (BN Jun 14 1929).

Those who came to see Bob in the first half of the week could immediately compare him with the German-American dog star, who was in the main film *Rinty of the Desert*. Later in the week the most intriguing item on the screen was without doubt *The Man Who Changed His Mind*, a drama produced by the Boy Scouts of Altrincham High School.

BN Oct 11 1929

"SPECIAL NOTICE   The Management take pleasure in announcing that they are installing, at considerable expense, one of the Latest Electrical Instruments, which produces Orchestral Music, so that their Patrons may enjoy the same standard of Entertainment as that presented by the Leading London Cinemas. This wonderful instrument will accompany all Films, commencing on THURSDAY, FRIDAY AND SATURDAY NEXT WITH *THE MERRY WIDOW* Featuring Mae Murray."

This film had previously been shown Sep 27–Oct 2 1926, but audience enjoyment was no doubt enhanced by the "Phantom Orchestra" as Mr Shepherd enthusiastically called his new piece of equipment.

It is interesting to note that a number of silent film versions of operas, operettas and musical comedies were shown at the Electric Palace between 1926 and 1929, including *The Bohemian Girl, Chu Chin Chow, The Waltz Dream* (with augmented orchestra under musical director W. H. Clifford), *The Count of Luxembourg, Rose Marie.*

Mon Dec 9 1929

"The annual Mayor's Christmas Fund benefit performance at the Electric Palace on Monday night was as enthusiastically patronised as ever. Full 'houses' were delighted with both the screen and concert programme arranged by the popular manager of the Palace, Mr Sydney C. Shepherd, and thoroughly appreciative of the spirit which prompted the directors in their generous effort to assist the Mayor in providing the poor of the town with yule-tide cheer.

At the close of the interval allotted to local artistes the Mayor (Councillor W. H. Powell) expressed his thanks to the directors of the Electric Palace for so kindly giving the benefit performances, to Mr Shepherd for his splendid effort in arranging such an excellent entertainment, and to the artistes who were always ready to come forward in the cause of charity. He also thanked the public for their attendance in such large numbers. The needs of the fund were as great as in any previous year and in supporting it they were helping to provide much needed Christmas comfort to many who through illness, old age and unemployment would otherwise be unable to afford any little luxury so dear at Christmas-tide.

Sustained applause greeted the efforts of the local performers, who made their appearances following the showing of the chief picture, 'The Conquering Power', which featured the late Rudolph Valentino, and Alice Terry. Particularly delightful was the artistic dancing of Miss Dulcie Gibbs' pupils, and Miss Marjorie Nunn, while the vocal efforts of Mr S. Bartlett and Miss Ethel Hutchings in duet met with unstinted approbation. Mr Joe Reed gave two well rendered solos and received his usual quota of encouragement ... As a result of the performances the Mayor's Christmas Fund will benefit by £18 15s" (BN Dec 13).

The Conquering Power was "presented in response to the request of many Patrons for a Valentino picture". It had been shown at the Palace in Barrack Street in May 1923. Valentino had died of peritonitis at the age of 31 on Aug 23 1926.

Thu Feb 20 to Sat Feb 22 1930

Showing of *A Peep Behind the Scenes*, a romance of life in a travelling fair, with Frances Cuyler and Haddon Mason. Produced by the British and Dominions Film Corporations Ltd and directed by Jack Raymond, who was born in Wimborne, this film had been made almost entirely in Dorset, with many scenes shot in the Bridport Fair field during the October Fair of 1928. Most of the shooting in Bridport had been carried out late at night and had inevitably attracted the interest of local residents. (See BN Oct 5 1928.)

During 1930 the Electric Palace showed a number of the new sound films in silent versions, e.g. *Show Boat* ("the magnificent silent version of this wonderful talking film"), *Broadway* (ditto), *The Virginian, Blackmail* ("a 'silent' version of the tremendously successful British 'talking' film, produced by Alfred Hitchcock"), *The Return of Sherlock Holmes* (starring Clive Brook, shown in Bridport Dec 11–13, then in Lyme Regis with sound Jan 8–10 1931).

Mon Nov 24 to Sat Nov 29 1930

The Cinema, Lyme Regis, presented its first talkie: *Sunny Side Up* (US 1929), an 80-min b/w musical featuring Janet Gaynor and Charles Farrell – America's Favorite Lovebirds – and some excellent songs, including I'm a dreamer; Keep your sunny side up; If I had a talking picture of you. The Electric Palace was to show this film just over two years later, Jan 5–7 1933.

The National 'Bus Company ran a special 'bus after the show on Saturday night to Charmouth, Morcombelake and Bridport – chars-a-banc were run during the week.

To counter the strong attraction of talkies at Lyme Regis the Electric Palace could offer that week Laura La Plante in a silent version of a mediocre all-talking romantic comedy *Hold Your Man*, and (more potent, perhaps), Garbo in MGM's last silent film *The Kiss*, directed by Jacques Feyder. No doubt quite a few Bridport cinema-lovers made their way over to Lyme in the last few weeks of 1930.

BN Dec 12 1930

"In order to keep abreast with the times, a policy which has always been adopted by the management of the Bridport Electric Palace, the latest in modern improvement the talking pictures are to be included in the programme early in the new year.

The equipment to be installed is British throughout, being manufactured by the British Thomson Houston Company. The selection of the B.T.H. sound producer was only arrived at after exhaustive tests and demonstrations of the various other apparatus on the market. The B.T.H. Company, as is well known, are the foremost electrical experts in Europe, and claim to be the only concern in this country that manufacture the whole of the apparatus contained in its 'talkie' set, from the iron amplifier case right through to the valves.

Two new 'Kalee' film projectors are also being installed. Here again is something entirely British made, being manufactured by Messrs Kershaw and Sons, of Leeds. Having accomplished this at considerable expense, the management now feel confident that they are in a position to present patrons with a high-class and up-to-date entertainment. It is with this object in view that the proprietors have based their future policy.

Talking pictures will commence on January 12th, with 'Rookery Nook' on the first three days, and 'Broadway Melody' on the last three days."

Mon Dec 15 1930

Two benefit performances were given as usual in aid of the Mayor's Christmas Fund. The entertainment on stage included character songs by Mr Frank Trevett and dances by Miss Dulcie Gibbs, Miss Marjorie Nunn and their pupils. "Each item was warmly applauded, and particularly pleasing was a vocal duet given with vivacity by little Delphine and Keith Abbott, or Dorchester, pupils of Miss Nunn" (BN Dec 19).

The main film of the evening was *The Flying Fleet*, starring Ramon Novarro, "a wonderful drama of love and friendship among the thrills of naval aviation". This was the first film to use location shots taken on board an aircraft carrier – the U.S.S. Langley.

Sat Jan 10 1931

The silent film era in Bridport came to an end with a final showing of *Welcome Danger*, a 110-min Harold Lloyd comedy, which itself reflected the transition, having been completed as a silent then almost entirely reshot as a talkie. Earlier in the week patrons had been enjoying the pantomime "Sinbad the Sailor", written and produced by Lionel B. Edwards and presented by a specially selected London company.

Just seven weeks after the Lyme Regis cinema, the Palace was about to go over to "talking" pictures, the proprietors having decided to do everything possible "to bring this popular house of entertainment right up-to-date and equal to the best talking picture theatres in the country" (BN Jan 9 1931).

From 1926 to 1931 the Electric Palace in South Street gave Bridport audiences the chance to see a wide variety of films, many of them trivial, slight and eminently forgettable, but quite a few of some value and interest and of more than just historical importance. Indeed, thanks to enterprising management, most of the outstanding films of the period were shown in the town.

Some major films were shown for a whole week:

1926   *The Merry Widow* (Sep–Oct); Chaplin's *The Gold Rush* (Oct – "secured at enormous expense")

1927   *Mons* (Sep–Oct); King Vidor's *The Big Parade* (Oct – anti-war, and the biggest grossing silent film of all); *Mademoiselle from Armentieres* (Nov), with Estelle Brody in the title role, a now forgotten British film made entirely by ex-servicemen and presented "with orchestra and effects"

1928   *Ben Hur* (Jan); *Beau Geste* (Mar – P. C. Wren's most famous novel had appeared in 1924); *What Price Glory?* (Apr), Raoul Walsh's humorous, realistic depiction of men in war, with Captain Flagg (Victor McLaglen) and Sergeant Quirt (Edmund Lowe) in pursuit of Charmaine (the delectable Dolores Del Rio); *7th Heaven* (Oct), with Janet Gaynor and Charles Farrell, the Screen's most perfect picture – presented at all evening performances with a song prelude by two popular local vocalists (Mr and Mrs T. Thear) and the orchestral accompaniment as played at the New Gallery Theatre, London

1929   Chaplin's *The Circus* (Apr); as second feature *Shoulder Arms* (May), "re-issued and presented by popular request"

1930   *The Trail of '98* (Sep), with Dolores Del Rio involved this time in the Klondike gold rush – "the greatest screen success since Ben-Hur"

All the great stars of the silent screen were seen at the Electric Palace, including:

Douglas Fairbanks in *The Thief of Bagdad*, *Don Q Son of Zorro*, *The Black Pirate*, *The Gaucho* ("How do YOU pronounce The Gaucho? Everyone pronounced it EXCELLENT"), *The Iron Mask*

Mary Pickford   in *Little Annie Rooney*, *Sparrows*, *My Best Girl*

Rudolph Valentino in *The Eagle, Cobra, The Son of the Sheik, The Conquering Power*

Alice Terry   in *Mare Nostrum, The Garden of Allah, The Conquering Power, The Prisoner of Zenda*

Buster Keaton   in *Go West, Battling Butler, Steamboat Bill Jr, The Cameraman, Spite Marriage*

Lillian Gish   in *Way Down East, La Boheme, The Scarlet Letter, Annie Laurie*

Laura La Plante in *The Midnight Sun, Her Big Night, Poker Faces, The Cat and the Canary, The Last Warning, The Love Trap, Show Boat, Hold Your Man*

Clara Bow (the "IT" Girl) in *Kid Boots, Wings, The Fleet's In, Dangerous Curves, The Wild Party*

Ivor Novello   in *The Bohemian Girl*, Hitchcock's *The Lodger, The Triumph of the Rat*, Hitchcock's *Downhill, The Vortex, The Constant Nymph*

Lon Chaney   in *The Unholy Three, The Road to Mandalay, While the City Sleeps*

Joan Crawford   in *Old Clothes, The Duke Steps Out, Untamed, Rose Marie*

Norma Shearer   in *Nothing to Wear, The Devil's Circus, The Mask of Comedy, The Student Prince, The Last of Mrs Cheyney*

Greta Garbo   in *The Temptress, Flesh and the Devil* ("The Screen's Most Passionate Drama, Stolen Moments of Blazing Passion. Are they worth the accruing Hours of Pain and Remorse? Solve this question by Seeing this Picture"), *The Divine Woman, The Kiss*

Ramon Novarro in *Ben Hur, Romance, The Student Prince, The Prisoner of Zenda, The Pagan, The Flying Fleet*

Ronald Colman in *Her Sister from Paris, Lady Windermere's Fan, Beau Geste, Two Lovers*

John Gilbert   in *The Big Parade, La Boheme, Flesh and the Devil, The Cossacks*

Constance Bennett in *The Code of the West, The Goose Woman, Should a Woman Tell?*

Dolores Del Rio in *What Price Glory?, Resurrection, Ramona, Revenge, The Trail of '98*

Harold Lloyd   in *For Heaven's Sake, The Kid Brother, Speedy, Welcome Danger*

Emil Jannings   in *Vaudeville, Faust, The Way of All Flesh, The Last Command*

Other stars, well known at the time but not previously mentioned, who appeared on the Bridport screen were:

Richard Arlen, Betty Balfour, Vilma Banky, John Barrymore, Noah and Wallace Beery, Madge Bellamy, Carlyle Blackwell, Betty Blythe, Chili Bouchier, Evelyn Brent, Carl Brisson, Jack Buchanan, Alice Calhoun, Eddie Cantor, Mary Carr, Syd Chaplin, Mady Christians, Lew Cody, Betty Compson, Fay Compton, Gary Cooper, Dolores Costello, Lili Damita, Marion Davies, Marguerite de la Motte, Richard Dix, Isobel Elsom, Hoot Gibson, Liane Haid, Mildred Harris, Lilian Harvey, Phyllis Haver, Jean Hersholt, Matheson Lang, Flora Le Breton, Bessie Love, Mona Maris, Moore Marriot, Shirley Mason, Adolphe Menjou, Tom Mix, Colleen Moore, Harry Myers, Pola Negri, Anna Q. Nilsson, George O'Brien, Sally O'Neill, Mabel Poulton, Aileen Pringle, Irene Rich, Lillian Rich, Stewart Rome, Pauline Starke, Vesta Sylva, Norma Talmadge, Conway Tearle, Fred Thomson, Glenn Tryon, Virginia Valli, Florence Vidor, H. B. Warner, Claire Windsor, etc.

Several distinguished Continental films came to South Street, there being, of course, no language barrier.

From Germany:

1927   *Vaudeville*, in which middle-aged trapeze artiste Jannings is betrayed by sexy Lya de Putti

1928   *The Emden*, produced under the aegis of the German Admiralty – The Thrilling Story of the Famous German Raider, the Romance of a Member of her Gallant Crew, and her Final Defeat by H.M.A.S. "Sydney" under the command of Admiral Glossop (that final defeat had taken place off the Cocos Islands in the Indian Ocean on Nov 9 1914; Admiral J. C. T. Glossop had given a lecture on the Destruction of the Emden in the Town Hall on Tue Dec 12 1922; see also Jun 7–9 1917); *Manon Lescaut*, with Lya de Putti and a relatively unknown Marlene Dietrich; Murnau's *Faust*, with Jannings as Mephisto

1929   Fritz Lang's *The Spy*, with Willy Fritsch; *Love's Crucifixion*, with Olga Tschechowa, "a thrilling and dramatic mother-love story, with the snowy wastes of Russia as a background"

1930   *Hungarian Rhapsody*, with Fritsch and Lil Dagover; *Volga Volga*, with Lillian Hall-Davis and Hans Schlettow; Fritz Lang's fascinating vision of the future, *Metropolis*, which made a star of Brigitte Helm

From Italy:

1927   *The Last Days of Pompeii*, directed by Carmine Gallone, the third Italian version of Bulwer Lytton's 1834 novel

From France:

1927   *The Gay Cavalier*, set in Louis XV's France and played by a cast of the foremost actors and actresses of France; a two-part version of *Les Misérables* (I The Soul of Humanity, II The Barricades), directed by Henri Fescourt

1928   *Bohemian Love*, starring Ivan Petrovich, "a well constructed love story with strong characterisation and an appeal specially to ladies" – "the picture is uplifting, dramatic, intensely human, and true to life, even though it savours now and again of a volatile life which is peculiarly French"; an excellent version of Mérimée's (not Bizet's) *Carmen*, with Raquel Meller, directed by Jacques Feyder

1929   *Prince of Adventurers*, with Ivan Mosjoukine as Casanova

From Denmark (Nordisk Films):

1928   *The Golden Clown*, with its Swedish stars Gösta Ekman (who played Faust in Murnau's film) and Karina Bell, "the Alma Taylor of Sweden" (Alma Taylor was the star of a number of throughly English films directed by Cecil Hepworth between 1915 and 1923. She was voted the most popular British star in 1915 and in 1925 was runner-up to Betty Balfour).

Manager Sydney Shepherd continued the policy he had established in Barrack Street of showing films of major sporting events, principally horse races and prize fights such as Dempsey v. Tunney (1926) and Scott v. Sharkey (1930). These supplemented the regular newsreel, Pathé's Super Gazette, which was replaced for a year (from early 1929 to Mar 3 1930) by Gaumont Graphic. Other documentaries and topical films of local/general interest appearing in the programme – besides those mentioned already – include:

1926 A series called *The Open Road* – a motor tour from Land's End to John O'Groats in the wonderful new all-British Friese-Greene Natural Colour Process

The official film of the Prince of Wales' Tour Round the World, in two parts. Mr Shepherd had managed to persuade Captain Charles Erard RN, who had accompanied the Prince, to give at each showing a descriptive talk on his experiences and the scenes depicted in the film, which was presented in July. The tour of Nigeria, South Africa, Argentina and Chile had taken place in 1925

Special film of the funeral of Rudolph Valentino in New York on Mon Aug 30 1926 – shown Sep 9–11

1927 Evolution or Was Darwin Right?

Film of the local Territorials at camp at Preston – shown in Sep with *The Last Days of Pompeii*

1928 Film of the funeral of the late Earl Haig, shown Feb 16–18 – he had died on Jan 30 at the age of 66

1930 The Departure and Disaster of the Ill-fated R101; The Lying in State and Funeral of the R101 victims. The R101 had crashed early on Sunday morning Oct 5 1930 on its maiden flight to India, killing 48 of the 54 passengers and crew, including the Air Minister, Lord Thomson, and almost all the airship experts of the Air Ministry. This disaster caused the Government to scrap the successful R100, designed by Barnes Wallis, and end airship development. The films were shown on Oct 16–18 and Oct 23–25.

Occasionally the management allowed the cinema to be used by a charitable organisation out of normal hours, e.g. on the afternoon of Tue Feb 5 1929 lifeboat films were shown free of charge, with a collection taken for the RNLI.

Leonard Stembridge's shop at 35 South Street about 1910, and the coalyard on which the New Electric Palace was to be built 1925/26 (see page 34).

The Bridport Electric Palace, Barrack Street, May 24 1912 (see page 3).

The Bridport Electric Palace, Barrack Street, June 1922. The posters are for A Woman of No Importance (GB 1921), a silent version of Oscar Wilde's 1893 comedy with Fay Compton and Milton Rosmer (showing Mon Jun 12 to Wed Jun 14) and The Woman God Changed (US 1921), a splendid Paramount production directed by Robert Vignola and featuring Seena Owen and an All-Star Cast (showing Thu Jun 15 to Sat Jun 17).

The staff at the Electric Palace, South Street, c. 1930. Among those standing are Sydney Shepherd (far right), commissionaire Bill Scaddens (centre) and William Ryan (third from the left).

Sydney Charles Shepherd 1884-1968.

An Orchestrion similar to that installed at the Electric Palace, South Street, in October 1929 (see page 48).

View of the Palace from the South Street car park, February 1997. As with most cinemas the exterior is unprepossessing.

The façade, c. 1950.

The façade, May 1997.

The entrance, November 1996. Note that the first N of ENTRANCE is upside down.

The main doors and former box-office extension, November 1996.

Murals by George Biles:

in the foyer, behind the counter

in the foyer, viewed from the stairs to the circle

on the stairs

on the stairs

on the stairs

towards the top of the stairs. The portrait of Paramount star Bob Hope in the circle foyer has been displayed in the cinema since the late 1930s.

The auditorium.

The commemorative plaque in the foyer, unveiled by the Mayor on June 14 1996
(see page 111).

Bridport (Electric) Palace, South Street

II From Monday January 12 1931 to Saturday September 2 1939

Mon Jan 12 1931

Having installed British Thomson Houston Co. equipment, the Electric Palace presented its first talking picture with sound: *Rookery Nook* (GB 1930), "an excellent British production adapted from the famous stage farce and featuring the original Aldwych Theatre cast, including Tom Walls, Ralph Lynn and Winifred Shotter" – and Robertson Hare. Directed by Tom Walls and Byron Haskin and made for £14,000, it ran for 76 minutes and was a great box-office success, grossing £150,000 in Britain alone.

The BN Jan 16 1931 included a report on the start of this new era: "Talking pictures were successfully inaugurated on Monday last and patrons were unanimous in their praise of the excellence of the reproduction ...

The opening picture was 'Rookery Nook' ... It was brimful of laughter and often the dialogue was drowned by hearty outbursts by a crowded house, but when the audience was not rocking with laughter every syllable could be heard distinctly in all parts of the hall. Mickey Mouse 'the king of cartoon-land' also had a great reception." (This b/w Disney cartoon, *The Plowboy*, was shown throughout this first week.)

Being a comedy, *Rookery Nook* demonstrated immediately and forcefully one of the disadvantages of the sound film, namely, that with comic dialogue screen actors cannot wait until laughter from the audience has subsided before continuing to speak – a problem that had not arisen with the visual humour of such masters as Linder, Chaplin and Keaton. (See also Sun Nov 2 1947.)

On Thursday, as usual, the programme changed to *The Broadway Melody* (US 1929), MGM's first All Talking, All Singing, All Dancing film, starring Anita Page and Bessie Love. It had been presented with the 1928/29 Best Picture Academy Award on Apr 3 1930, the first musical to be voted Best Picture. (The very first Best Picture Oscar – for 1927/28 – had gone to *Wings*, shown at the Electric Palace in Sep 1929.)

There was no change in the prices of admission.

With the advent of the talkies, the management announced in the advertisement BN Jan 9 1931 a revised and extended schedule of special buses leaving the Palace as follows:

EVERY NIGHT – Mr Smith to Burton Bradstock after the Last Performance

WEDNESDAY ONLY – National 8.15 to Bradpole, Loders, Chideock, Morcombelake, Charmouth and West Bay

SATURDAY NIGHTS – National to above districts at 8.30 and after Last Performance

SATURDAY NIGHTS – Mr Smith to Burton Bradstock 8.15 and after Last Performance

WEDNESDAYS AND SATURDAYS ONLY – Messrs Edwards & Hann from Beaminster at 5.35, leaving the Palace at 8.20

Edwards & Hann in their own advertisement (Special Cinema 'Bus Service) indicated the changes in their timetable, made "to enable our Customers to visit the 'Talkies'."

The schedule was modified from time to time, e.g. Mr Smith restricted his Burton Bradstock service to Wednesdays and Saturdays only early in February, and there was additions, e.g. from late March:

SATURDAYS ONLY – A Late Train leaves Bridport 8.55 for Powerstock, Toller and Maiden Newton

and from mid-April:

SATURDAYS ONLY – Mr Laver to Berwick, Swyre, Bexington and Puncknowle after Last Performance.

This special bus and train information for Palace patrons continued to be published until Feb 1 1935.

Mon Feb 23 to Sat Feb 28 1931

The first talkie to be shown for a whole week: *Rio Rita* (US 1929), starring Bebe Daniels and John Boles, a 135-min b/w and Technicolor version of the 1927 stage hit, the first Broadway musical to be successfully adapted for the screen.

The first British talkie to have a week's run (Sep 28 to Oct 3 1931) was *City of Song* (GB 1930), a 101-min musical about a young English socialite (Betty Stockfield) who holidays in Naples and falls in love with her Italian guide, played by the distinguished Polish tenor Jan Kiepura. "No British film has yet given us anything so beautiful."

A total of 16 feature films were booked for a whole week during this period (compared with 19 at the Lyric), and three films were brought back for a further three days soon after their first presentation. For details of these popular films see pages 64, 65 and 69.

Mon Aug 10 to Wed Aug 12 1931

Showing of the film version of *Lord Richard in the Pantry* (GB 1930, 95 min), the successful farce produced by the Bridport Amateur Dramatic Society in the Electric Palace four years earlier, on Mar 1 and Jul 22 1927.

Mon Sep 14 to Wed Sep 16 1931

Production by a specially selected London cast of the much discussed play "Potiphar's Wife", in which a Countess becomes infatuated with her chauffeur.

No other plays were presented at the cinema during the 1930s.

Mon Jan 4 to Wed Jan 6 and Mon Jan 11 to Wed Jan 13 1932

Two touring companies with specially selected casts of London artists brought pantomimes to the Palace stage, namely "Humpty Dumpty" and "Robinson Crusoe". One annual pantomime on stage in January continued as a regular feature on the programme up to the Second World War – including another "Robinson Crusoe" (1936) and two "Aladdins" (1933, 1939).

Thu Mar 17 1932

Showing at 3 p.m., under the patronage of the Mayor, of a film of life at Fairbridge Farm School, Pingarra, W. Australia, for British children, including the visit by the Duke and Duchess of York during their Empire Tour. Free, with a collection.

As in the "silent" period, there were occasional non-commercial events of this kind outside normal hours. Further examples: the two showings on Apr 19 1934 at 11.15 and 2.45 of *Through China and Japan*, produced by the Missionary Film Committee, and a very successful concert on Sun Sep 23 1934 at 3 p.m., arranged by Mr Joseph Lewis, one of the musical directors of the BBC, in aid of the Parish Church Organ Fund. (His widowed mother lived in Bridport.) The singers were Olive Townend (soprano), Freda Townson (contralto), Parry Jones (tenor) and Kenneth Ellis (baritone) – all well-known BBC artists – accompanied on the piano by Charles Webber and the composer Haydn Wood.

Thu Apr 7 to Sat Apr 9 1932

On the stage the fourth production of the Bridport Amateur Operatic Society: "The Gondoliers" – as usual three evening performances plus a Saturday matinee.

After their 11th (prophetic?) production in the Palace – "Goodnight Vienna" in Feb 1939 – the BAOS finally decided on "The Maid of the Mountains" for their April 1940 offering, but, as the BN reported in the Oct 6 1939 issue, the Committee were subsequently of the opinion that owing to the outbreak of hostilities it would not be possible to undertake another production during the war, so "The Maid of the Mountains" was postponed indefinitely – as it happened, till 1952. The Society's first post-war production in April 1947 was "The Gondoliers", for six days (not three) and in Church House (not the Palace).

Thu Jun 2 to Sat Jun 4 1932

Showing of *Men Like These* (GB 1931, 46 min), "a brilliant film of the heroism of the British submarine service", directed by Walter Summers and based on the true story of the submarine "Poseidon" which sank after being in collision with a battleship. The BN noted that "one cannot but feel that it was inspired by a recent naval disaster, as a tribute to the heroism of the men concerned in it".

On Tue Jan 26 1932 the submarine M2 had disappeared off Portland during exercises with the loss of 60 officers and men.

Compare the "Thetis" disaster of June 1939 in Liverpool Bay, and the excellent 1949 film *Morning Departure* with John Mills (inevitably) and Richard Attenborough, mainly produced at Portland Dockyard and shown at the Lyric in July 1951.

BN Jul 15 1932

"BRIDPORT ELECTRIC PALACE REDECORATED

Bridport's cinema, which enjoys a wide circle of popularity, and is acknowledged to be one of the finest little theatres in this part of the country, both architecturally and acoustically, has, during the past few weeks, been in the hands of the decorators.

The scheme consists of a set of six large panels and four smaller ones showing pastoral scenes painted in pastel shades with flat oil colours. These panels, which are nearing completion, have been designed and executed entirely by Mr F. G. Biles, a partner in the local firm of Messrs Cast and Biles, who secured the contract and who has earned for himself a reputation for pictorial sign work not only in Dorset but the two adjoining counties.

The panel surrounds are carried out in a soft shade of buff, while the ceiling and frieze have been finished with a pale putty tint, and the whole has been enriched with gold filigree work. The contractors are to be complimented on the success they have achieved, which will be more fully appreciated when it is realised that the normal running of the cinema was not interfered with.

We feel sure that the efforts of the Directors of the Palace will be readily appreciated by the people of Bridport. Perhaps not town of its size can boast a cinema so modern in all respects – an interior pleasing to the eye, modern lighting (new fittings are to replace the present ones) and acoustic properties of high standard, where one can be assured of spending an entertaining evening with one's favourite 'talkie' stars."

In an article on "The Art of the Modern Signwriter" in Town and Country News Jul 8 1932 featuring the firm of Messrs Cast & Biles of 71 East Street, it is noted that the new panels in the Palace "give the place an air of luxurious restfulness".

Biles' work was seen again in the cinema two years later when he designed and painted the scenery for the BAOS production of "The Pirates of Penzance" in April 1934. The BAOS continued to benefit from his skills in subsequent years.

The panels in the auditorium were unfortunately painted over in the 1950s.

All these attractive additions to the amenities of the Electric Palace were, surprisingly, never referred to in its BN advertisements.

BN Sep 30 1932

Announcement by the Palace management that "for the further convenience of Our Patrons the Performances will, in future, be TWICE NIGHTLY at 6 and 8.10, commencing Monday next, October 3rd".

This turned out to be not such a good idea, and in the BN Feb 3 1933 the management disclosed that "in response to the request of a large majority of Patrons" continuous performance would be restored on Mon Feb 6 except for Saturdays and Bank Holidays.

Seat prices at the Electric Palace

From early October 1932 these were: Front Stalls 7d, Centre Stalls 1/-, Back Stalls 1/6, Dress Circle 2/-.

From the end of June 1935 the price of the Front Stalls reverted to what it had been in 1926, 6d.

At the beginning of January 1937 a slight rearrangement of prices was announced: Dress Circle 2/- and 1/6, Back Stalls 1/6, Centre Stalls 1/-, Second Stalls 9d, Front Stalls 6d.

When the Lyric opened in December 1934, its seat prices were 6d, 9d, 1/- and 1/6. In early September 1935, in response to the Palace price reduction, the cheapest seats dropped to 5d.

Mon Dec 5 1932

This evening's performances – with the added attraction on stage of The Marionettes – were in aid of the Mayor's Christmas Fund, a tradition unaffected by the arrival of the talkies.

In 1933 in addition to the films Miss Dulcie Gibbs' pupils appeared on stage; in 1935 The Red Aces Dance Band performed, and in 1936 Ada's Rhythm Boys' Band and Mr E. S. Rimer, Entertainer. There appears to have been no live entertainment augmenting the film programme in 1934, 1937 and 1938.

The Second World War brought an end to this annual event.

The Lyric Cinema contributed similarly to the Fund between 1935 and 1937.

Good Friday Apr 14 1933

Beginning at 7 p.m., the Bridport Philharmonic Society gave a performance of Haydn's "Creation" in the Electric Palace. Immediately after the oratorio the Rector of St Mary's (the Rev. Lindsay Bartlett) "gave an interesting lantern lecture, entitled: The Cross and Passion of Our Lord Jesus Christ. The Parish Church Choir, occupying seats in the orchestra well, sang a series of hymns and other selections bearing on the slides. The audience also engaged in congregational singing" (BN Apr 21 1933).

Mon May 8 to Wed May 10 1933

Showing of the 1932 sound version of *The Lodger*, with Ivor Novello repeating the role he played in the classic Hitchcock 1926 silent film, presented at the Electric Palace in Aug 1927.

Mon Jun 12 to Wed Jun 14 1933

Second presentation of *Looking on the Bright Side*, Gracie Fields' first big film hit, "owing to the film's late arrival on its previous presentation" (Mar 9–11).

In late Feb 1936 there was a revival as second feature of Jessie Matthews' fifth film *The Midshipmaid*, first shown at the Electric Palace in Jun 1933, while Gracie Fields' fourth film *Love, Life and Laughter* reappeared in Dec 1938, having first been seen in Jan 1935. Laurel and Hardy's *Fra Diavolo* was also revived in Aug 1939, more than five years after its first showing in Bridport. Cicely Courtneidge's *Aunt Sally* is a further example.

This practice became more frequent during the Second World War, with the comparative shortage of new films and the increased demand of special Sunday programmes.

Fri Nov 30, Sat Dec 1 and Mon Dec 3 to Wed Dec 5 1934

Showing of special film of the Royal Wedding, i.e. of Princess Marina and the Duke of Kent on Thu Nov 29 at Westminster Abbey.

For the initial two days it accompanied Bridport's first sight of the incomparable Ginger Rogers and Fred Astaire as they launched their great partnership dancing the Carioca in RKO's *Flying Down to Rio*.

Mon May 20 to Wed May 22 1935

Showing of the British film *Little Friend* (Cert A, 85 min), starring Matheson Lang and 15-year-old Nova Pilbeam, "the problem of unhappiness and its effect on a sensitive child". The management recommended "that Children should not be brought to see this film", presumably because in it young Felicity attempts to commit suicide by gassing herself, thereby reuniting her divorcing parents.

A similar recommendation was made in Dec 1937, when another British film, the suspense drama *Love From a Stranger*, with Ann Harding and Basil Rathbone, came to the Electric Palace.

Thu May 23 to Sat May 25 1935

Pathe Pictures Ltd presents A Glorious Epic of the Reign of their most gracious Majesties King George V and Queen Mary entitled *Twenty-Five Years a King*, compiled with the collaboration of Rt Hon. Sir Austen Chamberlain, KG, PC, MP, and John Drinkwater.

"The Thrill of a Lifetime. This Cavalcade of Empire gets one by the throat" (Sunday Graphic).

A fortnight before, the Palace had shown the film of the Royal Jubilee Procession, and eight months later (Jan 30 to Feb 1 1936) its programme included The Royal Funeral Procession through London and Final Scenes at Windsor, King George V's life having moved peacefully to its close at Sandringham on Jan 20.

Thu Aug 8 to Sat Aug 10 1935

Variety show on the stage: The Romance of the Musical Hall, with Billy Cotton and his Band and well-known artistes, including Nellie Wallace and The Houston Sisters (Renée and Billie).

In 1938 another High-Class Variety Company took over the Palace for three days (Thu Oct 27 to Sat Oct 29). The turns included Samson (The Strongest Man on Earth), Tiny Rhodes, Clown Foyle and Dog Tex (Fun on a Staircase), Bud Ritchie (conversational comedian) and Margaret and Joan (the girls with the educated feet) – not quite up to the 1935 standard!

These shows, exceptionally, replaced the film programme, but live entertainers etc. were occasionally brought in, as during the silent period, to augment what was offered on screen, namely:

Thu Sep 19 1935 Parade of Mannequins (direct from London) displaying the Latest in Day, Dinner and Evening Gowns. Presented through the agency of M. M. Bonfield, West Street, Bridport

Mon Oct 14 to Wed Oct 16 1935 Evelyn Hardy, England's Greatest Lady Trumpeter, and her Ladies' Band of 12 brilliant musicians each playing at least two instruments

Mon Oct 19 to Wed Oct 21 1936 The Tele Robot. It sees. It hears. It speaks. It thinks. Is it Man? Is it Woman? Is it Human at All? The most amazing Electric Novelty of the Age. Amusing! Astounding! Uncanny!

Mon Nov 9 to Wed Nov 11 1936 Rema & Reta – Melodious Sensationalists. Solid Entertainment with a thrill.

Mon Aug 12 to Wed Aug 14 1935

Accompanying a minor musical *Transatlantic Merry Go Round*, starring Jack Benny, was Sir Alan Cobham's Film of a Lady Parachutist Jumping from Aeroplane. Tickets for a Free Flight awarded each Evening to Patrons giving correct distance of Jump.

Cobham's Great New Air Display, offering high speed and formation aerobatics, Miss Naomi Heron-Maxwell (the famous Parachute Girl, in Pull-Off Descents and Free Jumps), the "wingless" Autogiro, Passenger Flights in the "Astra" Giant Air Liner etc., took place at Dowlands Farm, Rousdon, Lyme Regis on Mon Aug 19 1935.

The following July/August, during the week's run of Eddie Cantor's *Strike Me Pink*, a number of free tickets were given away to Patrons, entitling the holder to a Free Flight in one of Mr C. W. A. Scott's Three-Engined Air Liners at the Air Display at Lyme Regis on Aug 6 1936. Scott had won the MacRobertson air race to Australia in Oct 1934 and was to win the race to South Africa in Oct 1936.

BN Oct 4 1935

The Electric Palace changed the format of its advertisement, with PALACE placed vertically down the left-hand side and SOUTH STREET (Phone 167) BRIDPORT along the top. This striking style, however, was soon abandoned to be replaced by a more traditional horizontal heading BRIDPORT ELECTRIC PALACE on Nov 8.

BN Mar 20 1936

The Electric Palace began experimenting with a series of slogans in its weekly advertisements: Palace means entertainment; Palace for Particular Picturegoers; Palace means entertainment in/plus comfort; Palace for sound pictures at their best; Palace means Bridport's own cinema – and, for the summer months from Jun 26: It's delightfully cool at the Palace.

The experiment was abandoned after Aug 7.

Sat Sep 19 1936

During the first house on Saturday night RSPCA Bronze Medals were presented by the Mayor to Mr Hyde and Mr Sylvester.

A similar ceremony took place on Sat Jun 12 1937, when the Mayor presented RSPCA certificates to Mr T. Butt, Mr F. Butt and Mr W. Murless for rescuing a dog from West Bay Cliffs.

The main film that evening was *Dimples*, one of the five Shirley Temple vehicles shown in 1937.

Thu Dec 10 to Sat Dec 12 1936

The climax of the abdication crisis, with Edward VIII relinquishing the throne on Dec 11. It is interesting to note that the films showing at this time in South Street were *She*, an American version of Rider Haggard's novel about the formidable Ayesha, She-Who-Must-Be-Obeyed ("Young and beautiful for 500 years – and wicked every one of them!"), and the final chapter of the serial *Call of the Savage*.

Earlier in the year King Edward was seen on the Palace screen unveiling the Canadian War Memorial at Vimy Ridge (Jul 30–Aug 1), at the Cenotaph (Nov 16–18) and visiting Weymouth and Portland (Nov 19–21).

Sat Jan 2 1937

This Saturday morning at 10.30 there was a special matinee for children of *Follow the Fleet* (with Fred and Ginger), at which a souvenir photograph of Shirley Temple was given to all children attending. The following Saturday, the children had another extra matinee at 10.30 to see Shirley in *The Littlest Rebel*, and when *Captain January* arrived in early March, they were able to see it at 10.15 on Sat Mar 4.

The Lyric Cinema, too, had organised special Shirley Temple children's matinees in Feb, Sep and Oct 1936 when presenting *The Little Colonel*, *Our Little Girl* and *Curly Top*.

On Sat Mar 26 1938 at 10.15 there was an extra matinee for children with the laudable aim of introducing them to the life of *Victoria the Great* (Anna Neagle in one of her best roles).

Mon Feb 22 to Wed Feb 24 1937

Showing of *The Country Doctor* (US 1936), featuring the Dionne Quintuplets – all girls – in a fictionalized version of their early days.

They were born in Ontario on May 28 1934 and appeared also in two sequels, *Hearts in Reunion*, shown Mar 7–9 1939, and *Five of a Kind*. A short documentary about them, *Going on Two Years*, had been shown Jun 11–13 1936.

Mon May 17 to Wed May 19 1937

Showing of a film of local celebrations of George VI's coronation, shot by Mr C. R. Hider, Photographer, South Street, Bridport. During the previous three days Palace patrons had been able to see a full-length film of the ceremony and procession in London.

Thu Sep 16 1937

"GIFT OF MEMORABLE FILM

A film of the Coronation ceremonies in London, reposing in a sealed container to maintain its preservation, was presented to the town of Bridport on Thursday evening by the General Film Distributors Ltd.

The ceremony took place at the Electric Palace during the first performance at which there was an exceptionally large attendance of the general public. A similar unsealed copy, running well over half an hour, was included in the programme.

The Mayor (Councillor H. R. C. Palmer), who accepted the gift, was accompanied on the platform by the Deputy Mayor (Alderman A. R. Travers, MBE), the Town Clerk (Mr S. Edgar Howard), Mr G. A. Morey (a director of the Electric Palace) and Mr W. Dovey (representing General Film Distributors Ltd).

Mr Dovey said the film was intended for the archives of the borough so that their children's children in generations to come would have an opportunity not only of reading in history of the Coronation, but also the opportunity of seeing and hearing it. A parchment with the film would probably be framed and hung in the Mayor's parlour or in one of the municipal buildings.

The Mayor said Bridport was exceedingly honoured to receive a copy. Only 20 were distributed among towns in Wales and the South-West and only five seaside resorts along the coast received one. To Mr Dovey and his firm they owed the greatest thanks. The parchment, he added, would be framed and placed in the museum.

Alderman Travers said the occasion was unique and one of which the town should be proud. He expressed thanks to the directors of the cinema for allowing the interesting ceremony to take place there" (BN Sep 24 1937).

The main film that evening was *Fire Over England*, a stirring account of the defeat of the Spanish Armada with a splendid cast, including Flora Robson, Laurence Olivier, Leslie Banks, Vivien Leigh, Raymond Massey, James Mason and Robert Newton.

Thu Nov 11 to Sat Nov 13 1937

Showing of *Our Fighting Navy* (GB 1937, 75 min, Cert U) about a British ship sent to a South American country to protect the British consulate against revolutionaries – "recently filmed at Weymouth with full cooperation of the Admiralty", and with two well-known American actors in the cast (Richard Cromwell and Noah Beery).

The film reappeared in Jan 1940, described as "an extremely typical and inspiring picture of the British Navy in all aspects of its lawful occasions", which was to exaggerate somewhat its quality and impact.

Thu Dec 1 and Fri Dec 2 1938

Cadbury Bros of Bourneville took over the Electric Palace to present their free film show: Cadbury Cavalcade. Patrons were encouraged to obtain tickets from their grocer or confectioner.

Thu Jun 1 to Sat Jun 3 1939

Accompanying the main feature *Listen Darling* (with 16-year-old Judy Garland and 14-year-old Freddie Bartholomew), and films of the Derby and Their Majesties' Arrival in Canada, was

The Warning A Message of National Importance. "This film, fully endorsed by Cabinet Ministers and public men of all parties, is in the nature of a timely warning to British citizens anent the possible peril of enemy air raids if suitable precautions are not taken to combat the grim effects of aerial invaders" (BN Jun 2 1939).

Sat Sep 2 1939

The last programme of peacetime at the Electric Palace was, rather suitably, an all-British double bill: *Hold My Hand*, a 75-min farce with Stanley Lupino, Fred Emney and Sally Gray, and *Meet Mr Penny*, a 70-min film version of a popular radio series, with Richard Goolden, Kay Walsh, Vic Oliver, Hermione Gingold and Wilfrid Hyde White.

A week before, again rather suitably, the main feature was entitled *Stand Up and Fight*.

As in the "silent" period, patrons of the Electric Palace in the years leading up to the Second World War were able to see most of the best entertainment films produced by the Hollywood and British studios and enjoy the performances of the great and popular screen actors and actresses of the time. Some weeks, of course, were less rewarding than others, and a good many of the films presented have been justifiably forgotten. However, in most years there were some 25–30 worthwhile films on view.

From Dec 14 1934 the Lyric Cinema in Barrack Street provided a further source of entertainment, so that a keen film fan in Bridport with sufficient funds and time could, if he or she wanted, see up to eight films a week, plus newsreels, shorts, cartoons.

The following 16 films were shown at the Electric Palace for a whole week:

1931   *Rio Rita* (Feb); *Whoopee* (Aug), another Broadway musical, starring the remarkably – if surprisingly – popular Eddie Cantor, "supported by a cast of

400", and with a hit title song immortalised later on screen by Michelle Pfeiffer on top of Jeff Bridges' piano in *The Fabulous Baker Boys* (shown at the Palace in Jul 1990); *City of Song* (Sep–Oct); Lubitsch's *Monte Carlo* (Dec), music, romance and comedy with Jack Buchanan and Jeanette MacDonald and "Beyond the Blue Horizon", memorably sung aboard the Blue Express

1932   *Daddy Long Legs* (Mar), "a Beautiful, Sentimental, but wholly Delightful Story of a Modern Cinderella and Her Millionaire Prince", i.e. Janet Gaynor and Warner Baxter

1933   *Cavalcade* (Nov), a US version of Noel Coward's 1931 stage success, with an excellent British cast (Clive Brook, Diana Wynyard, Ursula Jeans, Frank Lawton etc.) – winner of the 1932/33 Best Picture Oscar

1934   *The Kid From Spain* (Feb); *Roman Scandals* (Dec) – both with Eddie Cantor

1935   *Kid Millions* (Dec) (predictably): Cantor plus Ethel Merman and Ann Sothern

1936   *The Milky Way* (Jun), a Harold Lloyd comedy; *Strike Me Pink* (Aug) – Cantor and Merman again; *Modern Times* (Aug), a Chaplin masterpiece; *Things To Come* (Aug–Sep) – H. G. Wells, splendid sets and a fine score by Arthur Bliss

1937   *Show Boat* (Mar), with Paul Robeson singing "Ol' Man River"

1938   *Snow White and the Seven Dwarfs* (Nov – Cert A)

1939   *The Citadel* (Jun), King Vidor's version of A. J. Cronin's bestseller, with Robert Donat as the doctor

In all, three British and 13 American films, comprising two comedies, four dramas and ten musicals (five with Eddie Cantor).

[N.B. One or two of Disney's Silly Symphonies were kept for a week, e.g. *The Three Little Pigs*, with its catchy song "Who's Afraid of the Big Bad Wolf?" in Jul 1934.]

Three films were brought back for a second three-day run shortly after their first showing on account of their popularity, namely:

The House of Rothschild (US 1934), starring George Arliss with Loretta Young, Boris Karloff and C. Aubrey Smith – first shown Mar 28–30 1935, then "by request of many patrons", Apr 29–May 1 1935

The full-length film of George VI's Coronation – May 13–15 and May 20–22 1937

Victoria the Great, with Anna Neagle and Anton Walbrook – May 24–26 and Jun 27–29 1938

Films with popular British stars of the 1930s were well represented in the programmes at the Electric Palace, e.g.

Madeleine Carroll   *The Crooked Billet* 1/31, *Young Woodley* 6/31, *The W Plan* 7/31, *French Leave* 9/31, *The School for Scandal* 11/31, *I Was a Spy* 2/34, *Sleeping Car* 3/34, *The 39 Steps* 3/36, *Secret Agent* 4/37, *On the Avenue* 12/37, *Lloyd's of London* 12/37, *The Prisoner of Zenda* 8/38, *Blockade* 4/39

Ronald Colman   *Bulldog Drummond* 4/31, *Raffles* 8/31, *Arrowsmith* 8/33, *Bulldog Drummond Strikes Back* 5/35, *Clive of India* 11/35, *Under Two Flags* 12/36, *The Prisoner of Zenda* 8/38

George Arliss   *Disraeli* 7/31, *The House of Rothschild*, *The Millionaire* 6/35, *The Iron Duke* 6/35, *Alexander Hamilton* 8.35, *Cardinal Richelieu* 2/36, *Dr Syn* 5/38

Jack Buchanan	*Monte Carlo* 12/31, *Goodnight Vienna* 11/32, *Yes, Mr Brown* 9/33, *That's a Good Girl* 6/34, *Brewster's Millions* 9/35, *Come Out of the Pantry* 5/36, *This'll Make You Whistle* 7/37, *The Sky's the Limit* 6/38, *Smash and Grab* 10/38, *Break the News* 1/39
Cicely Courtneidge	*The Ghost Train* 4/32, *Jack's the Boy* 2/33, *Soldiers of the King* 8/33, *Falling for You* 1/34, *Aunt Sally* 8/34 and 4/36, *Things Are Looking Up* 8/35, *Me and Marlborough* 1/36, *Take My Tip* 12/37
Anna Neagle	*Goodnight Vienna* 11/32, *Bitter Sweet* 5/34, *Nell Gwyn* 5/35, *Peg of Old Drury* 3/36, *The Three Maxims* 4/37, *Victoria the Great* 3 and 6/38
Gracie Fields	*Sally in Our Alley* 12/32, *Looking on the Bright Side* 3/33, *This Week of Grace* 8/34, *Love, Life and Laughter* 1/35 and 12/38, *Sing As We Go* 3/35, *Look Up and Laugh* 1/36, *Queen of Hearts* 10/36, *The Show Goes On* 1/38
Jessie Matthews	*The Midshipmaid* 6/33 and 2/36, *There Goes the Bride* 7/33, *The Man From Toronto* 8/33, *The Good Companions* 1/34, *Waltzes From Vienna* 8/34, *Friday the 13th* 10/34, *Evergreen* 11/34, *First a Girl* 5/36, *Head Over Heels* 7/37, *Gangway* 5/38, *It's Love Again* 3/37, *Sailing Along* 12/38, *Climbing High* 8/39
Charles Laughton	*The Private Life of Henry VIII* 6/34, *The Barretts of Wimpole Street* 7/35, *Les Misérables* 11/35, *Rembrandt* 1/38
Leslie Howard	*Secrets* 1/34, *Smilin' Through* 3/34, *Berkeley Square* 12/34, *The Scarlet Pimpernel* 1/36, *Pygmalion* 4/39, *Stand In* 5/39
Will Hay	*Those Were the Days* 12/34, *Dandy Dick* 11/35, *Boys Will Be Boys* 3/36, *Where There's a Will* 5/37, *Windbag the Sailor* 6/37, *Good Morning, Boys* 7/37, *Oh, Mr Porter* 6/38, *Convict 99* 12/38, *Hey! Hey! USA* 4/39, *Old Bones of the River* 6/39
Robert Donat	*The Count of Monte Cristo* 9/35, *The 39 Steps* 3/36, *The Ghost Goes West* 7/36, *Knight Without Armour* 1/39, *The Citadel* 6/39
George Formby	*No Limit* 6/36, *Keep Your Seats, Please* 8/37, *Feather Your Nest* 9/37, *Keep Fit* 8/38, *I See Ice* 9/38, *It's in the Air* 5/39
Binkie Stuart (Britain's answer to Shirley Temple)	*Moonlight Sonata* 11/37, *Our Fighting Navy* 11/37, *Rose of Tralee* 11/37, *Little Miss Somebody* 8/38, *Little Dolly Daydream* 11/38
Vivien Leigh	*Fire Over England* 9/37, *Dark Journey* 10/37, *Storm in a Teacup* 8/38
Margaret Lockwood	*The Beloved Vagabond* 8/37, *Owd Bob* 11/38, *Bank Holiday* 12/38

Other British films of note shown at the Electric Palace include:

1931   *Journey's End* – "A Picture no Britisher should miss" – shot in Hollywood; Hitchcock's *Murder*

1932   *The Great Game* – "The first British 'soccer' talkie", being the story of a young centre-forward who finds himself a victim of the transfer system – featuring John Batten and 22 well-known League Footballers

1933   *Thark* – classic Aldwych farce

1934   *Sorrell and Son; Man of Aran; Catherine the Great*

1935   *The Man Who Knew Too Much; Sanders of the River; Escape Me Never; Lorna Doone*
1936   *For Ever England* – John Mills' first major film role
1937   *Tudor Rose; Land Without Music; Elephant Boy; Wings of the Morning* – Britain's first Technicolor feature; *King Solomon's Mines*
1938   *Old Mother Riley* – the first of many
1939   *Alf's Button Afloat* – the Crazy Gang; *The Divorce of Lady X; The Drum; South Riding; Housemaster; The Ware Case*

Popular British dance bands of the time were featured in a number of pleasant musicals: Jack Payne's in *Say It With Music* 8/33 and *Sunshine Ahead* 9/36, Henry Hall and his celebrated BBC Dance Orchestra in *Music Hath Charms* 4/36, Harry Roy and his Band in *Everything is Rhythm* 10/37 and Ambrose and his Orchestra in *Kicking the Moon Around* 2/39. (The Lyric supplied the Jack Hylton Band in *She Shall Have Music* 7/36, and Ambrose again in *Soft Lights and Sweet Music* 9/36.)

The German actor Conrad Veidt became very popular in British films such as *Rome Express* 6/33, *I Was a Spy* 2/34, *The Wandering Jew* 5/34, *Jew Süss* 6/35, *The Passing of the Third Floor Back* 4/36, *Dark Journey* 10/37, *Under the Red Robe* 5/38.

The stars of 1930s' Hollywood were seen in South Street in some of their best and most popular films, e.g.

Jeanette MacDonald   *The Love Parade* 11/31, *Monte Carlo* 12/31, *One Hour With You* 3/33, *The Merry Widow* 8/35, *Sweethearts* 8/39

Marlene Dietrich   *Morocco* 12/31, *Dishonored* 11/32, *Shanghai Express* 2/33, *Blonde Venus* 10/33, *The Scarlet Empress* 2/35, *The Garden of Allah* 1/38, *Knight Without Armour* 2/39

Jean Harlow   *Hell's Angels* 12/31, *Platinum Blonde* 7/32, *Dinner At Eight* 4/34, *Red Dust* 5/34, *Blonde Bombshell* 7/34

Janet Gaynor   *Daddy Long Legs* 3/32, *The First Year* 7/33, *State Fair* 10/33, *A Star Is Born* 9/38

The Marx Brothers *Monkey Business* 8/32, *Duck Soup* 1/35

Laurel and Hardy   *Jailbirds* 9/32, *The Music Box* 4/34, *Fra Diavolo* 5/34 and 8/39

Constance Bennett *What Price Hollywood* 12/32, *Moulin Rouge* 11/34, *The Affairs of Cellini* 6/35, *Everything is Thunder* 5/37, *Service De Luxe* 8/39

Greta Garbo   *Mata Hari* 1/33, *As You Desire Me* 5/33, *Grand Hotel* 3/34, *The Painted Veil* 10/35

Clark Gable   *Hell Divers* 1/33, *Red Dust* 5/34, *Night Flight* 6/34, *Dancing Lady* 7/34, *Chained* 9/35, *Forsaking All Others* 10/35, *Call of the Wild* 5/36

Joan Crawford   *Letty Lynton* 5/33, *Grand Hotel* 3/34, *Dancing Lady* 7/34, *Chained* 9/35, *Forsaking All Others* 10/35

Barbara Stanwyck *The Bitter Tea of General Yen* 10/33, *Annie Oakley* 10/36, *Stella Dallas* 3/39

Katharine Hepburn *Little Women* 9/34, *Morning Glory* 9/34, *Sylvia Scarlett* 1/37, *A Woman Rebels* 3/38, *Quality Street* 5/38, *Stage Door* 3/39

Ginger Rogers and Fred Astaire *Flying Down to Rio* 12/34, *Top Hat* 8/36, *Follow the Fleet* 1/37, *Swing Time* 1/38, *Shall We Dance?* 4/38

Mae West   *I'm No Angel* 1/35

Shirley Temple	*Baby Takes a Bow* 1/35, *The Girl in Pawn* 3/35, *The Littlest Rebel* 1/37, *Captain January* 3/37, *Poor Little Rich Girl* 4/37, *Dimples* 6/37, *Stowaway* 11/37, *Wee Willie Winkie* 3/38, *Heidi* 8/38
Deanna Durbin	*Three Smart Girls* 9/37, *100 Men and a Girl* 7/38, *Mad About Music* 1/39, *That Certain Age* 5/39, *Three Smart Girls Grow Up* 8/39
Sonja Henie	*One in a Million* 12/37, *Lovely To Look At* 7/38

Other interesting and/or important American films shown include:

1931   *All Quiet on the Western Front* – "the greatest picture ever given to the world"; *The Taming of the Shrew* – the only film in which Douglas Fairbanks and Mary Pickford appeared together; *Abraham Lincoln*

1932   *City Lights; The Champ; Tarzan the Ape Man*

1934   *Tugboat Annie*

1935   *Cleopatra; Dames*

1936   *Becky Sharp; Magnificent Obsession; The Informer*

1937   *Little Lord Fauntleroy; Dodsworth*

1938   *Winterset*

1939   *Dead End; You Only Live Once; The Hurricane; Nothing Sacred; The Adventures of Marco Polo* – starring Gary Cooper, whose most significant films during this period were shown at the Lyric; *The Great Waltz*

A number of interesting short films and documentaries found their way into the pre-war Palace programmes, in addition to the fairly regular diet of Royal occasions and major sporting events (the Derby, the Grand National, the Cup Final, the Boat Race, World Heavyweight Championship fights etc.), e.g.

1936   The "Queen Mary" at Southampton; The Sailing of the "Queen Mary"; *BBC: The Voice of Britain*, a 60-minute documentary produced by the famous GPO Film Unit

1937   *Bottle Party*, 44 minutes of about a dozen of the best of the turns appearing at the Windmill Theatre, London – just the thing for an August Bank Holiday audience

1938   The National Town Criers' Championship contest

1939   The French President in London; *North Sea*, directed by Harry Watt, spotlighting the ship-to-shore radio service and centred on an Aberdeen trawler; The National Service Review in Hyde Park

At the very end of November 1935 the Lyric showed *Lawrence of Arabia*, "the resume of the Life of a Wonderful Personality, containing many original War Office Films of the Irak Campaign".

Lawrence had died in Bovington Camp Hospital on May 19 1935 from injuries received in a motor-cycle accident six days previously.

The programmes at the Lyric quite often featured films shown earlier at the Electric Palace and brought back by request, e.g. *The Ghost Train, The Good Companions, Evergreen, The Girl in Pawn, The Kid from Spain, Clive of India, The Scarlet Pimpernel, Nell Gwyn, Escape Me Never, Sanders of the River, The Count of*

Monte Cristo, No Limit, Mata Hari. There were also revivals of films first shown at the Lyric, e.g. *One Night of Love, Lives of a Bengal Lancer, Lost Horizon.*

However, the Lyric showed exclusively many major films of the time and thus complemented what was offered at the Electric Palace. Nineteen of these films were given a week's run:

1935   *Lives of a Bengal Lancer* (Sep); *David Copperfield* (Dec–Jan 1936)

1936   *Broadway Melody of 1936* (Jul); *Curly Top* (Oct); *A Tale of Two Cities* (Dec–Jan 1937)

1937   *Mutiny on the Bounty* (Jan); *Rose Marie* (Jan); *San Francisco* (Aug); *The Great Ziegfeld* (Oct)

1938   *Maytime* (Feb); *Captains Courageous* (Mar); *The Good Earth* (Apr); *Broadway Melody of 1938* (May); *The Firefly* (Aug)

1939   *A Yank at Oxford* (Jan–Feb); *Test Pilot* (Feb–Mar); *In Old Chicago* (Mar); *Alexander's Ragtime Band* (Jul); *Kentucky* (Jul)

Other notable films given a run of three – occasionally four – days at the Lyric include:

1934   *Footlight Parade*

1935   *Voltaire; Queen Christina; Twentieth Century; Manhattan Melodrama; The Thin Man; The Invisible Man; Ruggles of Red Gap; Bright Eyes*

1936   *The Sign of the Cross; The Crusades; China Seas; Anna Karenina; Captain Blood*

1937   *Desire; A Night at the Opera; Mr Deeds Goes to Town; It Happened One Night; Fury; The Plainsman; Romeo and Juliet; Camille; The Charge of the Light Brigade*

1938   *Lost Horizon; Night Must Fall; Way Out West; A Day at the Races; Souls at Sea; Topper; The Life of Emile Zola; Wells Fargo; Marie Walewska; Happy Landing*

1939   *Rebecca of Sunnybrook Farm; Kidnapped; Boys' Town; The Lady Vanishes; Too Hot To Handle; Keep Smiling*

On the evidence of the advertised programmes for the Electric Palace and the Lyric Cinema, it would appear that one or two well-known British and American films of the 1930s were not shown in Bridport during the years leading up to the Second World War, e.g. *King Kong* – although the inferior *Son of Kong* turned up at the Electric Palace in September 1934; *A Farewell to Arms; I Am a Fugitive from a Chain Gang; Forty-Second Street; The Gay Divorcée; A Midsummer Night's Dream; Jezebel; The Adventures of Robin Hood; Sixty Glorious Years.*

Bridport (Electric) Palace, South Street

III The War Years: From Sunday September 3 1939
to Wednesday August 15 1945

Immediately after Neville Chamberlain's broadcast at 11.15 on Sunday morning Sep 3 1939, informing the country that it was now at war with Germany, there were a number of brief official announcements, one of which was that all theatres and cinemas were to close in order to minimize the chances of a large crowd being killed by a single bomb. On Sat Sep 9 it was announced that places of entertainment in evacuation reception areas could now reopen until 10 p.m.

It would appear that the Electric Palace accordingly reopened on Mon Sep 11 with the programmes already arranged for the previous week, i.e. Mickey Rooney in *The Adventures of Huckleberry Finn*, then (Thu–Sat) *Let's Be Famous*, a lively British comedy with Sonnie Hale, Jimmy O'Dea and Betty Driver, plus a very minor Western *Trailing Trouble*.

Bridport News Sep 22 1939

At the end of the regular weekly survey of films at the Bridport Electric Palace was the news that "the Palace is now under the management of the Plaza Cinema, Dorchester".

BN Sep 29 1939

"'The Bridport News' was officially informed this week that the Bridport Electric Palace has been sold to the Dorchester Cinema Company, who, in future, will conduct its management."

In the same issue was a report of the proceedings on Mon Sep 25 of the General Purposes Committee of the Dorset County Council, when an application was made for a licence to open the Palace on a Sunday.

"On behalf of the Dorchester Cinema Company Ltd, Mr L. Herrick Collins applied for a Sunday license in respect of the new Palace Cinema, Bridport. He said that this cinema had not had a Sunday license before, but there were numerous other towns in the county where such facilities had been granted.

Bridport, he pointed out, had a population of 5,917, and licenses had been granted at Wareham, Shaftesbury, Blandford and Wimborne, which had much smaller populations. With perhaps the exception of Lyme Regis, Bridport was the only seaside town in the county which did not have such facilities.

He said that the cinema was formerly owned by a gentleman who had a number of other business interests and it was for that reason he had refrained from applying for a Sunday license.

On Sunday evenings in Bridport at present there were a considerable number of young people in the streets who stood about in groups, causing a certain amount of obstruction, and hung about shop doorways. The same thing had apparently caused a certain amount of trouble in the past. In 1937 there was comment by the magistrates and the police about the need to stop horse-play in the streets on Sunday evenings. He felt that Sunday cinemas would help in that respect.

Mr A. G. Clapp, Mayor of Bridport, supporting the application, said that many young people cycled from Bridport to Dorchester to attend cinemas on Sundays and did not get back until one or two in the morning.

He thought it much more desirable that they should have facilities in their own town. Personally, he was not a Sunday picturegoer and hoped he would always refrain, but as long as the cinemas did not interfere with the churches he thought that people should have the facilities.

In reply to Mr A. H. Edwards he said he was speaking personally and that the matter had not come before the town council.

Alderman A. Spiller also supported the application and agreed that at one time there had been rowdyism in the streets on Sundays.

No objections were offered and the license was granted."

[Note the American spelling of "licence" throughout.]

Sun Oct 1 1939

The Palace opened at 6.45 p.m. to the general public for the first time on a Sunday, commencing at 7 p.m. The inaugural programme consisted of *Port of Seven Seas*, a Hollywood version of Pagnol's "Fanny", with Wallace Beery on the Marseilles waterfront, and the Singing Cowboy Gene Autry in *Springtime in the Rockies*.

The following three Sundays the cinema opened for troops only at 5 p.m., for the general public at 7.15, but on Oct 29 the military received no special treatment and joined the civilian audience at 7 p.m. to see – as was to be often the case on a Sunday evening – a fairly ancient double bill, on this occasion the Three Mesquiteers in the 1937 Western *Heart of the Rockies* (also in the Oct 22 programme), and *Manhattan Melodrama* (US 1934), with Clark Gable, William Powell and Myrna Loy, famous for being the film Public Enemy No. 1 John Dillinger had just seen before he was cornered and shot in Chicago on Jul 22 1934. (The Lyric had originally shown it in June 1935.)

The special "troops only" showings were not revived.

BN Oct 6 1939

"Bridport Borough Magistrates granted an application made to them on Saturday by Mr A. W. Lyall of Messrs Milne and Co., Bridport, on behalf of the Dorchester Cinema Company, owners of the Electric Palace, Bridport, for a music license at the cinema from 4.30 p.m. to 10 p.m. on Sundays and 10 a.m. to 11.30 p.m. on weekdays, excluding Christmas Day and Good Friday."

Mon Nov 6 to Sat Nov 11 1939

The first film since the outbreak of war to be shown for a week: *The Little Princess*, Shirley Temple in Technicolor to brighten up a gloomy November.

The Lambeth Walk (GB 1939) opened on Boxing Day (a Tuesday) and continued for the rest of the week – a version of the cheerful and highly successful stage show "Me and My Girl" with Lupino Lane and Sally Gray. It returned for another three days at the Lyric in Jan 1941 and at the Palace in Sep 1943.

No other films were given an unbroken run of six days at the Palace during the war (though see entry on *Mrs Miniver*, below).

The Four Feathers was shown for a week at the Lyric (Jan 1–6 1940), as was *Stanley and Livingstone* (Apr 29–May 4 1940), but thereafter the mid-week change of programme remained the regular pattern for both cinemas.

Mon Dec 11 to Thu Dec 14 1939

The Technicolor film of *The Mikado* (GB 1939), with Martyn Green, other members of the D'Oyly Carte Company, and an American crooner Kenny Baker, was shown for four days, for the benefit of G & S fans deprived of BAOS productions for the duration of hostilities.

BN Jun 7 1940

With the Lyric Cinema now owned by the Dorchester Cinema Company, the first appearance of a joint advertisement for the Palace and the Lyric, plus an intervening and vertical DCC.

The weekly survey of films at the South Street cinema was still headed Bridport Electric Palace – the change to The Palace did not come until the issue of Jun 6 1941.

Mon Aug 19 to Wed Aug 21 1940

The Wizard of Oz reaches Bridport.

Thu Oct 3 to Sat Oct 5 1940

Showing with Max and Dave Fleischer's feature-length cartoon version of *Gulliver's Travels* was the excellent 18-min documentary *Men of the Lightship* (GB 1940), produced by the Crown Film Unit, the first and possibly the best of the British wartime films about the sea.

Thu Oct 10 to Sat Oct 12 1940

Showing of *Road to Singapore*, the first of the Bing Crosby/Bob Hope/Dorothy Lamour comedies with music. *Road to Zanzibar* followed in April 1942, *Road to Morocco* in June 1943.

Thu Dec 19 to Sat Dec 21 1940

Showing of *Britain Can Take It*, the shorter version for domestic distribution of Humphrey Jennings' and Harry Watt's fine 10-min film about people coping with the Blitz *London Can Take It*, aimed specifically at the Empire and American market, with commentary by Quentin Reynolds and music from Vaughan Williams' London Symphony.

Sat May 17 to Sat May 24 1941

Bridport and District War Weapons Week (target: £45,000), to which the Palace contributed in the following ways:

"Yet another act of liberality on the part of the directors of the Dorchester Cinema Company, who are the owners of the Palace, South Street, Bridport and the Lyric Cinema, is the gift of £50.

The whole of this generous sum will be allocated as prizes to school-children in Bridport and district during the local War Weapons Week. The prizes will take the form of Savings Certificates and all will have an equal chance to compete for them" (BN May 16 1941).

[It is interesting to note that in the previous year when the Bridport, Beaminster and District Spitfire Fund was launched on Thu Sep 19 1940, a representative of the

Dorchester Cinema Company had presented £20 to the fund at the opening meeting. It took 12 weeks for the target of £5,000 to be reached and surpassed.]

Some of the Ministry of Information's most successful productions were included in a special film programme which the Dorset Information Committee presented at the Palace on Thu May 22, starting at 3 p.m., admission free.

Under the title "Britain at Arms" the programme consisted of: "War and Order", "Her Father's Daughter", "Green Food For Health", "Behind the Guns", "Owner Comes Aboard", "All Hands" and "Britain at Bay", and it lasted 70 minutes; children under 14 were admitted only with an adult.

On Sat May 24 (Empire Day) Salute to Empire was presented at the Palace, beginning at 2 p.m., as the climax of War Weapons Week.

"On Saturday afternoon a pageant in dance and song entitled 'Salute to Empire' was staged in the Palace Cinema. Presented by Miss Compton and Miss Fairbairn it proved to be a delightfully colourful production, brilliantly executed and with deep patriotic appeal. The dances were arranged by Miss Fairbairn, of the Royal Academy, London, and the musical items were given by the Bridport Singers under the leadership of Miss Compton. Miss Dorothy Stone, ARCM, was at the piano. Others taking part were the private pupils of Miss Fairbairn, Bridport Keep Fit Class, The Youth Movement (Bridport Group), English Folk Dance Society (Bridport branch), the pupils of St Ronan's School, St Hilda's School, St Mary's School, Symondsbury School and Bridport General School (Senior and Junior)" (BN May 30 1941).

The Bridport News had described the planned programme earlier, in particular the finale:

"The concluding scene should be a most inspiring one, for it will be a tableau representing Britannia surrounded by her daughter nations, to the music of Vaughan Williams' new song 'England my England'. This magnificent song by our foremost British composer is likely to become our second national anthem. It has only just been written, and will receive its first performance somewhere in England on May 15, and its second by the Bridport Singers in Salute to Empire. At this moment it is not possible to say if the first performance will be broadcast, but it will be used as the theme song of Salute to Empire, and its recurrence will be the link which binds the daughter nations to the mother country. In the finale it will become a community song, and the whole audience will be asked to join in singing it. It should be a fitting climax to a remarkable show" (BN May 16 1941).

"At the close the Mayor warmly complimented Miss Compton and Miss Fairbairn on the outstanding success of the production. He also acknowledged the generosity of the directors of the cinema in allowing the use of the building free of charge" (BN May 30 1941).

£200,803 was raised during the Week.

Sun Jun 29 1941

Showing of "the most sensational film of the year", *Professor Mamlock*, a Russian film made in 1938 about a leading surgeon of a Berlin hospital in 1933, who is publicly degraded because he is a Jew. He is gunned down while making an impassioned speech against the Nazi régime.

Described in the BN advertisement as "a withering exposure of Hitlerism", the film was initially banned in Britain because of its anti-German stance (comparable to that of Eisenstein's *Alexander Nevsky*, made in 1938 also), but it became an excellent propaganda tool on the outbreak of war, one powerful and comprehensive enough at any rate to be given an evening's exposure in Bridport. It may have surprised that Sunday's audience, who were given no clue as to its origin and subject matter.

Only one other foreign film was shown at the Palace during the war, and this, too, hailed from Russia: a fascinating documentary *One Day of War*, shown from Thu Apr 22 to Sat Apr 24 1943, shot by some 160 Russian cameramen recording the activities on the entire Russian Front on Jun 13 1942. The management warned that "this film is not suitable for children" – the supporting feature *Old Mother Riley MP* was certainly not suitable for intelligent adults.

The Lyric showed a French film, *Double Crime in the Maginot Line*, on Apr 22–24 1940, but it was "a complete English-speaking version of the recent sensational French success". Audiences were told it was topical and gripping, and advised not to miss it; just over a fortnight later, on May 10, the Germans launched their Western Offensive, the phoney war was over and the Maginot Line proved to be utterly ineffectual.

Mon Nov 24 to Wed Nov 26 1941

Showing of *Target for Tonight*, Harry Watt's 48-min morale-boosting semi-documentary account of a raid on Germany by Wellington bombers, in particular "F for Freddie".

Sat Mar 21 to Sat Mar 28 1942

Bridport and District Warship Week – objective: £70,000, the cost of the hull of a large minesweeper. Total finally achieved: £169,117, to which the Palace management contributed by offering two special attractions at the cinema, namely:

On Mon Mar 23 at 6 p.m. and 8.15 p.m. a Tip-Top Stage Show – The Garrison Follies in "Night Lights".

"Jimmy Silver and his Band presented 'Night Lights' in a high-speed variety show at the Palace Cinema, where, through the generosity of the management, the whole of the proceeds were given to Warship Week fund.

Every seat in the building was occupied, and the large audience thoroughly enjoyed the efforts of this talented band of entertainers, all of whom are serving with H.M. forces" (BN Mar 27 1942).

On Thu Mar 26 at 6.30 p.m. a Grand Variety Concert, including:
The Choir of the Royal Welch Infantry Brigade
Miss Fairbairn presenting Bridport Children in a Dance and Song Scena "Great Britain and Her Allies"
The Bridport Ballet Club in "Les Sylphides"
Members of the Bridport Keep Fit Class in "Russia Dances"
Ernest Abbot, "The County Magician"
Bandsman L. Garcia and His Violin, with Bandsman C. Dean at the Piano (By kind permission of Bandmaster E. J. Webb, ARCM)

Miss Dulcie Gibbs presenting Pupils of the Malvina School of Dancing in "Dancing Kiddies" also "Eight Bells" (A Nautical Speciality).

Tickets for both Monday's and Thursday's shows were: Reserved seats 2/6, 2/-, 1/6, Unreserved 1/-. There were no reduced prices for children on the Monday evening.

BN Mar 27 1942
The Palace/Lyric advertisement included a "Special Notice: Owing to the Paper Control, no Posters will be exhibited until further notice.   Full particulars of Programmes see Local Press".
This notice appeared for the last time on May 1 1942.

Sun May 3 1942
On and from this date only the Palace opens on Sundays.

Sun Aug 2 1942
Shortly after 6.30 p.m. two Me 109s dropped bombs in the West Street area and machine-gunned the streets. Four people were killed.
"At the time the Palace cinema was crowded, yet few were aware of the danger until anxious friends made enquiries after the missiles had dropped" (BN Oct 6 1944).
The films then showing continuously from 5 p.m. were *A Bill of Divorcement* (US 1940), with Adolphe Menjou, Maureen O'Hara and a clutch of Hollywood British actors, and *Sued for Libel* (US 1939), "an efficient programmer".

During the Bridport and District "Dorsetshire" Replacement Week (Sat Sep 19 to Sat Sep 26 1942), which aimed to raise £168,000 in War Savings as part of a country-wide campaign, the Palace did not host any special events – a concert by local artistes took place in Church House.
H.M.S. Dorsetshire, which had delivered the coup de grâce to the "Bismarck" on May 27 1941, was herself sunk off Ceylon, together with H.M.S. Cornwall, by Japanese dive-bombers on Easter Sunday Apr 12 1942.

Mon Sep 28 to Wed Sep 30 1942
The showing of *Dangerous Moonlight* gave Palace audiences the chance to see Anton Walbrook and hear Louis Kentner playing Richard Addinsell's celebrated Warsaw Concerto – with the added bonus of the presence of Sally Gray.

Thu Mar 18 to Sat Mar 20 1943
Showing of *Queen Victoria*, a conflation of Herbert Wilcox's highly successful pre-war films *Victoria the Great* (presented at the Palace on March and June 1938) and *Sixty Glorious Years*.

Thu May 6 to Sat May 8 1943
Showing of the six-Oscar-winning *Mrs Miniver*.
Then, in the BN May 21 1943: "The Management take pleasure in announcing that they have secured a return booking of *Mrs Miniver* for the Lyric, Monday, Tuesday, Wednesday, June 7th, 8th, 9th" – with a matinee each day at 2.30; evenings continuous from 5.40.

BN May 14 1943

PLEASE NOTE! New Admission Prices come into force on SUNDAY NEXT. Circle, Front 2/9 Circle, Back 2/3 Back Stalls 2/3 Centre Stalls 1/9 Front Stalls 1/-. These prices applied to both cinemas

Sat Jun 5 to Sat Jun 12 1943

Bridport and District Wings for Victory Week – target: £60,000, the cost of a squadron of Spitfire fighters. Total raised: £105,400.

The Palace's contribution was a Grand Celebrity Concert on Sun Jun 6 at 2.30 p.m.

"Rich in musical talent was the pianoforte recital and concert given in the Palace Cinema on Sunday afternoon, when the artists included Miss Irene Kohler, one of the most brilliant of the younger pianists of the day, Miss Vera Florence, a soprano of considerable charm, and Mr George Baker, who excelled both as a singer and a speaker.

Mr Hugh Shirreff, of the R.A.F., and formerly one of the B.B.C. announcers, compered the show in a most pleasing manner, and Miss Dorothy Stone scored a personal triumph in accompanying the vocal items.

Applause, frequent and sustained, greeted each item in a varied programme that was a sheer delight to those privileged to enjoy it.

The gratitude of the audience and the organisers of the effort was expressed by the Mayor (Councillor S. J. Gale) who specially mentioned the help received from Dr and Mrs Ryan, of Burton Bradstock, in obtaining the services of the artists, and their cooperation in a variety of ways.

Bouquets were presented to the ladies taking part at the close of the concert, which the Mayor described as one of the most successful from a musical point of view ever held in the town" (BN Jun 11 1943).

The event raised £66 13s 6d.

That evening regular Sunday patrons were treated to typical dominical US fare: *They Dare Not Love* (Austrian prince v. the Gestapo) and *Henpecked* aka *Blondie in Society*. Quite a contrast with the afternoon entertainment.

Mon Aug 2 to Wed Aug 4 1943

First showing of *In Which We Serve* – "this is incomparably the finest film yet produced in a British studio".

It returned – rather incongruously – for two days towards the end of Salute the Soldier Week (Thu/Fri Jun 15/16 1944).

Thu Aug 12 to Sat Aug 14 1943

Showing of *Desert Victory*, the classic documentary account of the battle at El Alamein.

Other fine feature-length British documentaries shown at the Palace were *Close Quarters*, A Story of Britain's Submarines (Nov 29–Dec 1 1943), *World of Plenty*, on post-war food production and distribution (Feb 8–10 1945) and *Western Approaches* (May 24–26 1945).

The Lyric presented *Coastal Command* in Jan 1943 and *Tunisian Victory*, rather tardily, in Mar 1945, having earlier, in Jan 1942, introduced Bridport to *The World in*

Flames, an interesting American compilation of 1930s newsreel material about the rise of the dictators.

BN Oct 15/Oct 22 1943

The cinemas' advertisement carried the appeal: Please Support The Merchant Navy Comforts Service Campaign October 11th to December 11th, 1943.

This then changed (BN Oct 29/Nov 12/Nov 19/Nov 26) to: Please Support Bridport's Fund of Gratitude To The Merchant Navy October 11th to December 11th, 1943.

Mon Nov 15 to Wed Nov 17 1943

An outstanding programme: *Casablanca*, and Humphrey Jennings' *The Silent Village*, a moving 36-min re-enactment by the people of the Welsh village of Cwmgiedd of the tragic story of the Czech mining village of Lidice, obliterated with most of its inhabitants by the SS on Jun 10 1942 as a reprisal for the assassination of Reinhard Heydrich.

Wed Nov 24 1943

Two Grand Celebrity Concerts on stage, at 2.45 and 7.30. Admission: 7/6, 5/-, 3/6 and 2/6.

"Rich in musical talent were the concerts given in the Palace Cinema, Bridport, on Wednesday afternoon and evening, when the artistes taking part in the programmes were Miss Irene Kohler (pianist), Miss Olive Groves (soprano), Mr Geo. Baker (baritone) and Mr G. Wykeham-George (cellist). The accompanist was Miss Dorothy Stone, ARCM, of Bridport.

The effort was in aid of the Merchant Navy Comforts Fund, and at the close of the evening performance the Mayor (Councillor S. J. Gale) announced that the objective which Bridport and the district had set out to obtain, namely, £500, had already been exceeded. An attempt would now be made until the middle of next month to double this amount.

During the interval the Mayor was presented with a cheque for £25 2s as the amount raised in a competition, the prize for which was a doll given by Miss Pamela Shepherd, daughter of Mr S. C. Shepherd, manager of the Palace Cinema. There were over a thousand entries, and the winner was a Beaminster woman.

Miss Shepherd was assisted in the competition by friends and pupils of St Ronan's School, Bridport" (BN Nov 26 1943).

The amount raised by these concerts was £153 2d.

1944 opened rather dully as far as the Bridport cinema programmes were concerned. During the month of January, according to the BN advertisements, 21 films were shown at the Palace – eight of them on Sunday – and 16 at the Lyric: a total of 37 films, none of which could be said to be of high quality. One or two, however, may have a certain historical interest, especially a record of a sitting of the B.B.C.'s Brains Trust with Commander A. B. Campbell, Dr Julian Huxley and Dr C. E. M. Joad, shown at the Palace in support of a recent British film *I'll Walk Beside You*, which featured the St David's Singers and the London Symphony Orchestra.

No doubt all or most of these minor features and programme fillers, some dating from the late 1930s, managed to entertain undemanding audiences of civilians and service personnel in the fifth winter of war and take their minds off more serious matters (such as the coming invasion of Northwest Europe) for an hour or two. Usually the film fare was a little more substantial, with each month bringing a few films of value and lasting interest.

Tue Jun 6 1944 – D-Day

The Palace had an Anglo-American programme: *The £100 Window* (GB 1943), a comedy-drama about gambling on the totalizator, with Frederick Leister, Anne Crawford and Richard Attenborough, and *Follies Girl* (US 1943), a third-rate b/w musical. The Lyric offered *Isle of Forgotten Sins* (US 1943), a melodrama about sunken treasure in the South Seas, and *No Place For A Lady* (US 1943), an uninvolving murder mystery, which reappeared later one Sunday in October 1945. Clearly, a day to stay in and listen to the wireless rather than go out to the pictures.

The £100 Window turned up at the Lyric in Oct 1945.

Sat Jun 10 to Sat Jun 17 1944

Bridport and District Salute the Soldier Week – target: £90,000, the cost of six Churchill tanks. Total raised: £121,500.

On Sat Jun 17 Gerald Savory's comedy "George and Margaret" was performed by the Wessex Players (an amateur company from the Wimborne district) in the Palace Theatre, "kindly loaned by the Proprietors for this Special Occasion of National Importance".

In his speech thanking the performers for the valuable contribution they had made the Mayor also "gave unstinted praise to the directors of the Dorchester Cinema Company, whose generosity in granting the free use of the cinema made the show possible under such ideal conditions. In turn he mentioned the management and staff and those who, in a variety of ways, had a part to play in what was undoubtedly one of the most successful productions ever staged in the town" (BN Jun 23 1944).

The play – matinee and evening performance – raised about £156. A 1940 British film version of it had been shown at the Palace Feb 13–15 1941.

BN Sep 29 1944

A surprise announcement in the middle of the Palace/Lyric advertisement: "We regret that owing to certain conditions placed upon us by the Dorset County Council, the Palace Cinema will not be open on Sundays as and from October 1st, until further notice". This announcement, minus "as and from October 1st", reappeared on Oct 6.

On the previous page of the BN there was an explanatory declaration by the Cinematograph Exhibitors' Association: "As a result of a decision by the General Purposes Committee of the Dorset County Council to increase the compulsory levy on Sunday takings, the Association has decided with regret that all CINEMAS IN DORSET WILL BE CLOSED ON SUNDAY, 1ST OCTOBER and until further notice".

The BN Oct 6 1944 contained the following article on the closing of Dorset cinemas on Sundays by Alan Maitland:

"By now, I suppose, the Dorset County Council will have received a telegram from the Lord's Day Observance Society congratulating them on the decisions which have led to the closing of all cinemas in Dorset on Sundays. They are hardly likely to have congratulations from anyone else.

The exhibitors have alleged that 'sabbatarian influences' are responsible for the Council's actions. How far that is true cannot, of course, be said, but the cinemas must have some basic evidence for such a statement, and, if such is actually the case, a serious stage of affairs will have been constituted.

If the county authority is to be so readily swayed by ridiculous and puritanical motives, at the behest of a narrow-minded few 'behind the scenes', there is no apparent limit to what might yet happen in Dorset on a Sunday. If a cinema performance is to be 'against the Sabbath', then we may as well stop all broadcasting and ban concerts and discussion groups. Unfortunately we will not be able to stop the war as well, and that is where the closing of the cinemas becomes an unnecessarily-imposed hardship.

Granted, Sunday performances have not always been of the most desirable kind. We have been inclined to have a little too much of Hollywood and a little too less of Ealing. But the important thing is that they have fulfilled a definite need. The attractions of the Dorset towns are such that to Service men and women in particular, the problem of what to do on a Sunday evening is a difficult one, and the advent of dark evenings does not make its solving any lighter.

Would the County Council wish rather that the public houses take the place of the cinemas, or that aimless groups should wander the streets? With the cinemas closed, however, what alternative does it suppose is left to the Servicemen in small towns like Bridport?

It will be seen that, while this business may be reasonable enough to the civilian, it is unjust and undeserved to those fighting for their country, to those who cannot withdraw into a Victorian atmosphere of heavy curtains, antimacassars and aspidistras, as a few apparently desire.

While the attempt of the D.C.C. to increase the 'tax' to a height which would have been crippling to the small owner may have had the best of intentions (though they are difficult to see), it has had, in fact, an entirely opposite effect, for with the trade's refusal to meet this demand en bloc, charity is now about to be something like £4,000 a year poorer. In addition to these two points there is added a third, concerning the children.

Considering the nature of most films shown by exhibitors, perhaps it is well that the under 16s should be kept away, but what is the sense of a regulation which seeks to forbid them on a Sunday but admits them on a weekday when, in many cases, the same film is still being shown?

The boredom of an English Sunday is detested by none more than the children, by whom it is generally acknowledged to be the worst day in the whole week. We know that from our own experiences when young, and perhaps some of us have even carried the dislike through the years. No one will deny that the children need brighter Sundays, too. A lot of nonsense has been and it being talked in juvenile courts concerning the much-abused film industry, and it has been blamed for juvenile delinquency, which has been proved to be untrue.

The fact is, of course, that the cinema can be a great educator, especially if the right type of films are shown. (Something after the style of 'A Canterbury Tale' is needed.) The exhibitors have proved their willingness to experiment in this direction, particularly the Odeon circuit (which, incidentally, has a stout Methodist as its chairman), but the Dorset County Council has, rather dictatorially, it seems to me, refused to consider all their suggestions for modification.

The decisions will be accepted with a great deal of regret and not a little anger from the general public and the Services, although no one will blame the exhibitors for standing up against what they consider to be an injustice. The County Council would do well to reconsider the whole question."

Note: Michael Powell and Emeric Pressburger's *A Canterbury Tale* was, unfortunately, not shown in Bridport. In fact, none of their major wartime films reached South or Barrack Street.

The military authorities made representations to the General Purposes Committee via the Weymouth Town Clerk, and the general pressure was such that in the BN Oct 13 1944 the Palace could announce that it would reopen on Sunday next, i.e. Oct 15, along with all the other Dorset cinemas. And this it did, enticing the briefly deprived audience with the traditional double bill: *No Time For Comedy* (James Stewart and Rosalind Russell) and *Ladies Must Live*.

Two members of the Dorset Regiment, Derek Hounsell and W. L. Love, wrote to the BN to express their thanks to Mr Alan Maitland for the criticism contained in his article: "We share his views in this matter and remember the many Sunday evenings when we, as members of H.M. Forces, have tried to find amusement in other towns where the Sunday ban has been in force" (BN Oct 20 1944).

Tue May 8 1945 – VE Day

The Palace was showing *The Hitler Gang* (US 1944), "The Truth about a Gang that Stole a Nation", an account of Hitler's rise to power from 1918 to 1934 (with Robert Watson impersonating the Führer) and one of the best of Hollywood's treatments of the Nazi phenomenon.

In Barrack Street the Lyric's patrons could see Anna Neagle in a 1936 British film *The Three Maxims*, a circus drama shown at the Palace in Apr 1937, plus *The Girl Who Dared* (US 1944, 56 min, b/w), memorable only for the fact that in it was Kirk Alyn, who was to play Superman in Columbia's 1948 15-part serial.

The BN May 11 1945 reported that "a free cinema show was given to the children of the town on Wednesday afternoon at the Palace, South Street". Presumably they weren't treated to Hitler and his henchmen.

Wed Aug 15 1945 – VJ Day

The Palace was showing *And Now Tomorrow* (US 1944), a sentimental tale in which deaf socialite Loretta Young is won by poor doctor Alan Ladd (returning to films after being invalided out of the USAAF), plus *The Singing Musketeer* (US 1939), a burlesque version of The Three Musketeers with songs from the Ritz Brothers, and a reminder, perhaps, of the early months of the war – it was first shown at the Lyric at the beginning of October 1939.

Rather typically, all the Lyric could offer was *Made For Each Other*, a 1939 tearjerker about young marrieds, with James Stewart and Carole Lombard (who had tragically died in an air crash early in 1942), first shown at the Lyric in Apr 1940. Supporting it was *The Man Who Wouldn't Die* (US 1942), 65 minutes of murder, blackmail and a wise-cracking detective.

A survey of the film programmes at the Palace and the Lyric during the war years reveals that:

- Bridport audiences were able to see a good many of the best and most entertaining films of the time – with, as might be expected, American movies easily outnumbering those from British studios. (In the five years 1940–44 the US made 2,255 feature films, the UK just 217.)
- A considerable number of films reappeared for a further three-day run or for a Sunday evening show (a few were revived more than once). The vast majority of these had been first shown before the war, in two cases as far back as 1933.
- The Sunday films (particularly to start with) were usually either fairly old or fairly undistinguished and unmemorable. Most of the better ones had already been shown in Bridport, but one or two notable films were exhibited on a Sunday only.
- A good many major British and American films made and/or released during the war were not shown in Bridport during this period – in some cases this is rather surprising.
- After 1940 the programmes at the Lyric were on the whole less interesting than those at the Palace, and the Lyric relied more heavily on revivals.

Major and/or popular British feature films shown at the Palace during the week

1939   *Vessel of Wrath, Trouble Brewing, The Mikado, The Lambeth Walk*

1940   *The Lion Has Wings, Jamaica Inn, Ask a Policeman, Poison Pen, Goodbye Mr Chips, The Four Just Men, Come on George, French Without Tears, Q Planes, The Spy in Black, Gaslight, Contraband*

1941   *Night Train to Munich, Charley's Big-Hearted Aunt* (Arthur Askey), *Freedom Radio, Gasbags* (the Crazy Gang), *The Ghost Train, The Prime Minister* (i.e. Disraeli), *Let George Do It, Convoy, Spare a Copper, The Ghost of St Michael's, Jeannie*

1942   *Major Barbara, Cottage to Let, Kipps, Quiet Wedding, Atlantic Ferry, South American George, Dangerous Moonlight, Unpublished Story, Alibi*

1943   *Much Too Shy, Thunder Rock, Thursday's Child, We'll Meet Again, In Which We Serve, Get Cracking, Tomorrow We Live*

1944   *My Learned Friend, Salute John Citizen, Bell Bottom George*

1945   *Medal for the General*

Major American feature films shown at the Palace during the week

1939   *Jesse James, The Hound of the Baskervilles*

1940   *Idiot's Delight, The Sun Never Sets, The Adventures of Robin Hood, Confessions of a Nazi Spy, Dodge City, Only Angels Have Wings, At the Circus* (Marx Brothers), *Sherlock Holmes, Babes in Arms, The Cat and the Canary, Ninotchka, The Women, The Wizard of Oz, Mr Smith Goes to Washington, Gulliver's Travels, Road to Singapore, Typhoon, The Blue Bird, Northwest Passage*

1941   *The Shop Around the Corner, The Ghost Breakers, Strike Up the Band, The Sea Hawk, Pride and Prejudice* ("Jane Austen's gay comedy"), *The Return of*

Frank James, Tin Pan Alley, Down Argentine Way (Betty Grable and Carmen Miranda), *The Road to Frisco* (i.e. *They Drive by Night*), *Chad Hanna*

1942 *The Flame of New Orleans, Northwest Mounted Police, Man Hunt, Road to Zanzibar, Love Crazy, I Wanted Wings* (plus Veronica Lake), *Honky Tonk, Penny Serenade, Hold Back the Dawn, Billy the Kid, Dr Jekyll and Mr Hyde, Two-Faced Woman* (Garbo's last film), *Blossoms in the Dust, You'll Never Get Rich* (Astaire and Hayworth), *Here Comes Mr Jordan, Babes on Broadway, Woman of the Year, Ladies in Retirement*

1943 *The Fleet's In, Reap the Wild Wind, Holiday Inn* (and "White Christmas"), *The Glass Key, Louisiana Purchase, Mrs Miniver, This Gun for Hire, For Me and My Gal, Road to Morocco, You Were Never Lovelier, The Major and the Minor, The Talk of the Town, Sergeant York, The Commandos Strike at Dawn, International Squadron, Across the Pacific, Casablanca, Yankee Doodle Dandy, Blues in the Night, The Man Who Came to Dinner*

1944 *Random Harvest, Presenting Lily Mars, Air Force, Mission to Moscow, Action in the North Atlantic, Watch on the Rhine, King's Row, Thank Your Lucky Stars, Lassie Come Home, Song of Russia, Thousands Cheer, Destination Tokyo, Now Voyager, Escape to Happiness, Madame Curie, A Guy Named Joe, This is the Army, Two Girls and a Sailor, The Seventh Cross*

1945 *The Murder in Thornton Square, My Friend Flicka, Bathing Beauty* (Esther Williams), *The Adventures of Mark Twain, Jane Eyre, Lady in the Dark, Going My Way, Double Indemnity, The Hitler Gang, Dragon Seed, For Whom the Bell Tolls, Cabin in the Sky, The White Cliffs of Dover, Hail the Conquering Hero, Old Acquaintances, 30 Seconds Over Tokyo, Frenchman's Creek*

Some films given a second run at the Palace (with year of first showing)

First shown at the Palace

1940 *Pygmalion* (1939), *Our Fighting Navy* (1937), *Wings of the Morning* (1937)

1942 *Trouble Brewing* (1939), *Vessel of Wrath* (1939)

1943 *Sleeping Car* (1934), *Peg of Old Drury* (1936), *Look Up and Laugh* (1936), *The 39 Steps* (1936), *The Lambeth Walk* (1939), *The Count of Monte Cristo* (1935), *Convoy* (1941)

1944 *Elephant Boy* (1937), *Sanders of the River* (1935), *Storm in a Teacup* (1938), *Random Harvest* (1944), *Rembrandt* (1938), *The Prisoner of Zenda* (1938)

1945 *Pride and Prejudice* (1941), *The Adventures of Robin Hood* (1940), *Quiet Wedding* (1942), *Nothing Sacred* (1939), *The Goldwyn Follies* (1939)

First shown at the Lyric

1943 *The Proud Valley* (1941)

1944 *Captains Courageous* (1938), *Rose Marie* (1937), *The Oklahoma Kid* (1940)

1945 *Captain Blood* (1936)

Major and/or popular British feature films shown at the Lyric during the week

1939   *I Met a Murderer, A Stolen Life, I Killed the Count*
1940   *The Four Feathers, Shipyard Sally, For Freedom, The Frozen Limits* (the Crazy Gang), *The Edge of the World, The Arsenal Stadium Mystery, Band Waggon, Dark Eyes of London* (Britain's first "H" certificate film)
1941   *The Green Cockatoo, The Stars Look Down, Pastor Hall, The Girl in the News, Sailors Three* (Tommy Trinder, Michael Wilding and Claude Hulbert), *The Proud Valley*
1942   *Sons of the Sea, The Night Has Eyes*
1943   *Hatter's Castle, Happidrome*

Major American feature films shown at the Lyric during the week

1939   *Angels With Dirty Faces, Suez, The Dawn Patrol, Algiers, The Cowboy and the Lady, Stagecoach*
1940   *The Oklahoma Kid, Topper Takes a Trip, Captain Fury, The Young in Heart, Second Fiddle, Beau Geste, Wuthering Heights, Made For Each Other, Union Pacific, Susannah of the Mounties, Stanley and Livingstone, The Man in the Iron Mask, Dark Victory, Juarez, The Rains Came, The Light That Failed, Destry Rides Again, Young Mr Lincoln, When Tomorrow Comes, First Love, The Real Glory, A Chump at Oxford, Dark Command*
1941   *My Little Chickadee, Tower of London, Go West* (Marx Brothers), *The Philadelphia Story*
1942   *The Big Store, H. M. Pulham Esq., When Ladies Meet*
1943   *Journey for Margaret, They Died With Their Boots On*
1944   *That Uncertain Feeling, Of Mice and Men*
1945   *Till We Meet Again, High Sierra, The Big Shot, The Male Animal, The Maltese Falcon*

Some films given a second run at the Lyric (with year of first showing)

First shown at the Lyric

1941   *David Copperfield* (1935)
1942   *I Killed the Count* (1939), *The Stars Look Down* (1941), *I Met a Murderer* (1939), *China Seas* (1936), *Lost Horizon* (1938), *The Lady Vanishes* (1939), *Fury* (1937), *Dark Command* (1940)
1943   *The Plainsman* (1937), *San Francisco* (1937), *G Men* (1936), *The Street Singer* (1937)
1944   *Stagecoach* (1939), *Lost Horizon* (1938, fourth appearance), *Topper Takes a Trip* (1940), *Captain Fury* (1940)
1945   *The Cowboy and the Lady* (1939), *Made For Each Other* (1940)

First shown at the Palace

1940   *Under Two Flags* (1936)

1941   *The Lambeth Walk* (1939), *The Ghost Goes West* (1936, shown Apr and Dec 1941), *It's in the Air* (1939), *Q Planes* (1940), *The Spy in Black* (1940)
1942   *Glamorous Night* (1938), *Love from a Stranger* (1937), *Good Morning Boys* (1937), *King Solomon's Mines* (1937), *The Spy in Black* (1940, again), *Brewster's Millions* (1935)
1943   *Take My Tip* (1937), *Ask a Policeman* (1940), *O.H.M.S.* (1937), *Thark* (1933), *Mrs Miniver* (1943), *Escape Me Never* (1935), *I See Ice* (1938), *Nell Gwyn* (1935), *There Goes the Bride* (1933), *Transatlantic Merry Go Round* (1935), *Catherine the Great* (1934), *Laburnum Grove* (1937)
1944   *Stand In* (1939), *Things to Come* (1936), *The Return of the Scarlet Pimpernel* (1938), *The Show Goes On* (1938), *Dreaming Lips* (1938), *Arms and the Girl* (1936), *All At Sea* (1940), *Ladies in Retirement* (1942), *Q Planes* (1940, again), *The Spy in Black* (1940, again)
1945   *Out of the Fog* (1943), *The Four Just Men* (1940), *Penny Serenade* (1942), *The Doctor Takes a Wife* (1941), *The Three Maxims* (1937), *Old Mother Riley* (1938)

A few of the better Sunday films

Already shown in Bridport

1940   *The 39 Steps*
1941   *Alf's Button Afloat, The Man Who Knew Too Much, Owd Bob*
1942   *Night Train to Munich, The Four Just Men, The Ware Case*
1943   *Only Angels Have Wings, The Ghost Goes West, Ladies in Retirement*
1944   *Billy the Kid, Honky Tonk, International Squadron*
1945   *San Francisco, Dr Jekyll and Mr Hyde, Ruggles of Red Gap, The Glass Key*

Not (apparently) shown in Bridport previously

1941   *Professor Mamlock*
1942   *My Favourite Wife, The Hunchback of Notre Dame, Balalaika*
1943   *A Woman's Face*

Major British and American feature films not (apparently) shown in Bridport during the war

British

The Thief of Bagdad, 49th Parallel, The First of the Few, The Foreman Went to France, Next of Kin, One of Our Aircraft is Missing, Went the Day Well?, The Young Mr Pitt, The Bells Go Down, Fires Were Started, The Gentle Sex, The Life and Death of Colonel Blimp, Millions Like Us, Nine Men, San Demetrio London, This Happy Breed, We Dive at Dawn, A Canterbury Tale, Fanny By Gaslight, I Know Where I'm Going, The Way Ahead, Henry V

American

Gunga Din, Gone With the Wind, Fantasia, Foreign Correspondent, The Grapes of Wrath, The Great Dictator, The Long Voyage Home, Pinocchio, Rebecca, Citizen Kane, Dumbo, How Green Was My Valley, The Little Foxes, Sullivan's Travels, Suspicion, That Hamilton Woman (featured on the British "100 years of going to the pictures" 25p stamp), *Bambi, The Magnificent Ambersons, Saboteur, Lifeboat, Shadow of a Doubt, The Song of Bernadette, Laura*

Some of the above-mentioned were to get a showing in Bridport after the war.

It is particularly surprising to find important and entertaining films from Powell & Pressburger, Hitchcock and Disney in these lists, but the presence of Orson Welles' first two movies is perhaps to be expected.

Bridport Palace, South Street

IV From the Age of Austerity to the Demise of the Lyric: Thursday August 16 1945 to Saturday September 1 1962

In 1946 cinema-going in the UK reached the peak of its popularity, with 31.4 million seats being sold per week. By 1956 weekly attendance had dropped to 21.2 million and six years later to just 7.6 million. The impact of television was the main cause of this decline, which was as evident in Bridport as elsewhere.

The general pattern of a mid-week change of programme continued at both the Palace and the Lyric throughout this post-war period, with a fair sprinkling of revivals. The practice of showing certain popular films for a six-day run was resumed, but the use of the Palace as a theatre was virtually restricted to the annual spring production of the BAODS. The X film and Cinemascope – the cinema industry's two major attempts to counter the competition from TV – found their way to Bridport in the 1950s, but the combination of horror and sex (in the latter case often imported from the less inhibited Continent), plus a little rock and roll from Haley, Presley, Steele and Co. and a couple of experimental Grand Repertory Weeks (with an entire change of programme each evening) in March and August 1960, was unfortunately not enough to save the Lyric.

Oct to Nov 1945

Showing of a quartet of very good American films: *Arsenic and Old Lace* (Oct 4–6), *Sunday Dinner for a Soldier* (Oct 18–20), *To Have and Have Not* (Nov 1–3), with Bacall telling Bogart how to whistle, and *Meet Me in St Louis* (Nov 5–7), with Judy Garland and The Trolley Song. Audiences in that rather drab first autumn of peace were no doubt delighted.

Mon Jan 14 to Wed Jan 16 1946

Churchill's favourite film *Lady Hamilton* (original US title *That Hamilton Woman*), starring Vivien Leigh and Laurence Oliver, finally reaches Bridport.

Sun Mar 16 1947

A 17-year-old patron steals an 18-year-old patron's navy blue overcoat from the cloakroom of the Palace. In its pockets are a blue bordered handkerchief and personal points coupons. The case is reported in the BN Apr 18 1947.

The film on that Sunday evening was *The Human Comedy*, first shown at the Palace in Feb 1944, a version of William Saroyan's novel about a small Californian town in WW2, expressing his optimistic view of the human race. As one critic wrote: see it and reaffirm your faith in people.

Mon Apr 7 to Wed Apr 9 1947

Appearance on the Palace stage at 5.35 and 8.15 of The Great Nixon, the World's Master Mind Reader, answering unseen written questions submitted by the audience – "The most Baffling Presentation ever seen on Stage or Screen". This Easter Holiday special attraction was in support of *Hats Off to Rhythm*, a very minor American musical, which certainly needed all the support it could get.

BN May 9 and 16 1947

A brief publicity campaign on behalf of British films begins with a photograph of Margaret Lockwood, saying (in a balloon to her left): "We can't grow tobacco but we *can* make films".

This statement is accompanied by the comment: "Britain spends £18,000,000 a year on American films. Let's see more *good* British films and save dollars".

Margaret Lockwood was replaced in the ...

BN May 23 and 30 1947

... by: "GOOD – it's a BRITISH Picture!" shown as if projected on a cinema screen and set against a background of British film titles. "Let's see more of them" interrupted the titles across the lowest section of the advertisement, which on May 30 was reduced in size.

During this period of four weeks the Palace and Lyric showed in all 35 films, five of which were British.

Thu Jul 17 to Sat Jul 19 1947

Showing of Howard Hughes' "much discussed film" *The Outlaw* (Cert U), a version of the story of Billy the Kid starring the curvaceous Jane Russell. "The film is a daring and stirring story of rugged romantic conflict. In addition to the proven elements of spectacular action and turbulent romance 'The Outlaw' has the added attraction of enticing Jane Russell, whose alluring physical assets have made her Hollywood's most talked-about film beauty" (BN Jul 11 1947).

Made in 1941, the film did not get a wide showing till 1950, when it was re-released by RKO.

Those more interested in car bodywork could go along to the Star Garage in East Street, where Goering's bullet-proof Mercedes was on show (Jul 14–19) in aid of the Bridport Hospital.

BN Sep 26 1947

"For this week-end the film 'Traffic With the Devil' is being shown at the Palace Cinema, Bridport. It is a revealing survey of the horrible toll in human lives occasioned by the ever-increasing use of motor transport.

The film, made in Los Angeles, the world's worst city for road deaths, dramatically indicts the many types of driver-offenders, presents stark close-ups of victims, and suggests remedies which may halt these appalling tragedies. It is a timely and salutary offering for every variety of cinema-goer. A human film, it evenly balances tears with smiles and horror with humour."

There was a separate advertisement for this 15-minute film, which the Bridport, Lyme Regis and District Road Safety Committee urged all locals to see. "You will see the good-time Charlie whose eyes are more on the curves of a blonde than on the winding of the street – the woman who inspects her make-up in the driving mirror at 50 m.p.h. – the people who are never wrong on the road. A crash, a fire, a trip in an ambulance – perhaps the last ride of all."

The main accompanying film was the artless, long and long-forgotten *When You Come Home* (GB 1947), starring the popular and vulgar Lancashire comedian Frank Randle.

Sun Sep 28 1947 to Sun Jan 16 1949

The Palace is the only cinema open in Bridport.

Sun Nov 2 1947

Showing of *Rookery Nook*, which older patrons might have seen first in Jan 1931, when it opened the talkie era at the Palace.

Sat Nov 22 to Wed Nov 26 1947

Showing of the film of the Royal Wedding (Elizabeth and Philip), which had taken place at Westminster Abbey on Thu Nov 20. On the Sunday it accompanied two familiar British films: *Look Up and Laugh* (1935, Gracie Fields) and *Nell Gwyn* (1934, Anna Neagle).

When *The Big Sleep* was presented the following week (Dec 4–6), there was a special attraction with it: *The Inside Story of the Royal Wedding*, told by Anna Neagle.

Mon Jun 21 to Sat Jun 26 1948

The first feature film since 1939 to be shown at the Palace all week: *The Best Years of Our Lives* (US 1946) – "The Most Honoured Picture in History. Presentation takes nearly three hours and you will want to see it more than once." This fine film deservedly won seven Oscars.

It reappeared at the Lyric for three days in Sep 1950 and again in Jun 1961.

According to the advertisements in the Bridport News, over this period of 17 years the Palace showed 59 films for a week – ten days in one exceptional case. Forty-one of these films were British, 18 American. The Lyric kept 22 different films in all for an extended run: ten British and 12 American. Of these 22, seven had already been seen in Bridport.

N.B. There were no BN advertisements in the six issues Jun 28 to Sep 22 1961 inclusive.

Mon Sep 20 to Wed Sep 22 1948

Claude Spencer, BBC Baritone-Entertainer, performs on the stage for 15 minutes each evening before the two showings of the main feature *To the Ends of the Earth* (US 1948), a well-made thriller about a world-wide chase after a narcotics gang.

Thu Oct 7 to Sat Oct 9 1948

Accompanying *Dick Barton – Special Agent* (GB 1948) is *Mate o'Mine*, Introducing Pan, the blind sheepdog, of Washingpool Farm, Bridport.

The BN of Jan 14 1949 contained the following explanatory article:

"The screening of the film at Bridport and in other towns in the West Country of 'Mate o'Mine', depicting the intelligence of dogs and their usefulness to man in many countries, has focussed attention on Pan, an 11-year-old blind Scotch border collie, one of the central figures in the film. She belongs to Mr F. White, of Washingpool Farm, Bridport, who recently was appointed Vice-Chairman of the Dorset County branch of the N.F.U.

Blindness overcame Pan three years ago, but despite this handicap she continues to tend and direct the large flock on Mr White's 150-acre farm with a dexterity and swiftness seldom surpassed by a normal sheepdog. She was awarded first prize in an open sheepdog trial at South Petherton two years ago and has also bred a number of prize-winning puppies, one of them gaining a second in a recent trial at Chard.

When Mr White appeared on the stage at a Yeovil cinema a few nights ago he told the audience that Pan loved to fetch the sheep with his cowman's son, eight-year-old Roy Gudge. 'People call Pan the "Pride of Dorset", and if she could only speak, she would be almost human'."

Mon Jan 3 to Wed Jan 5 1949

Showing of Powell and Pressburger's outstanding ballet film *The Red Shoes* (GB 1948), an excellent start to the new year. The Lyric revived it for three days at the beginning of September "in response to numerous requests".

The Palace showed two full-length films featuring the Bolshoi Ballet in Nov 1958 and Feb 1960.

BN Feb 18 1949

Attention is drawn – by a letter, an item in the Youth Forum section and a special advertisement – to a J. Arthur Rank short film on the Army Cadet Force, entitled *Look Ahead*, to be shown at the Palace during the week commencing Feb 21. "All interested in the ACF should see this film."

The Bridport company of the 1st Cadet Battalion, Dorset Regiment, was in need of new recruits between the ages of 14 and 18.

Thu Mar 10 to Sat Mar 12 1949

A warning is given to parents regarding the British gangster drama on show *No Orchids for Miss Blandish*: "Note. Patrons should not bring their children to see this film."

This is not surprising. Though the final script bore little resemblance to James Hadley Chase's bestselling shocker and though the film was passed by the British Board of Film Censors in March 1948 with an A certificate, critical and political opinion was scathing. For example, according to the BFI Monthly Film Bulletin "this must be the most sickening exhibition of brutality, perversion, sex and sadism ever to be shown on a cinema screen". Many local councils demanded cuts in the film, some watch committees banned it altogether.

The unfortunate Miss Blandish returned briefly to Bridport on Sun Sep 18 1955.

In Nov 1950, when the Lyric showed *The Snake Pit* (Cert A), starring Olivia de Havilland as a patient in a mental institution undergoing shock therapy, the management again saw fit to issue a warning, or rather, this time, a prohibition: "SPECIAL NOTICE – Children under 16 CANNOT be admitted whether or not they are accompanied by a parent or guardian". A few weeks later, in Jan 1951, the British Board of Film Censors introduced the X certificate to designate films unsuitable for juvenile audiences, and such special monitory notices became unnecessary.

Thu Apr 28 to Sat Apr 30 1949

After two post-war productions in Church House the Bridport Amateur Operatic and Dramatic Society returns to the Palace with four performances of "The Mikado", first produced by the Society at the Electric Palace in Feb 1929. "The seating, probably the most comfortable in Bridport, will enable nearly 2,000 people to see the play. Every seat will be bookable" (BN Apr 8 1949). All seats were sold by Mon Apr 25.

At the annual meeting of the BAODS in the Greyhound Hotel, reported in the BN Jul 22 1949, the Chairman, Mr J. Vernon Payne, remarked that "the return to the Palace was largely experimental. The cinema had been let to the Society at what must have been a 'very nominal' figure – less than was paid pre-war and that was very largely a gesture on the part of the directors of the Dorchester Cinema Company."

Thu Aug 25 to Sat Aug 27 1949
Showing of the third Royal Command Performance film *Scott of the Antarctic*, with its fine Vaughan Williams' score.

In this period all of the films thought fit to set before a king or queen – and some were fairly mediocre – were shown in Bridport except the first (and arguably the best) *A Matter of Life and Death* and the fourth *The Forsyte Saga*, which came to the Regent, Lyme Regis. The Palace was the preferred exhibitor, presenting ten of the 13.

Mon Oct 17 to Wed Oct 19 1949
Showing of *All Over the Town*, an enjoyable sub-Ealing comedy about corruption exposed by reporters on a West Country local newspaper. Starring Norman Wooland and Sarah Churchill, the film had been made at Lyme Regis (converted into Tormouth) during the summer of 1948.

The supporting feature was *Way Out West*, the Laurel and Hardy classic first seen in Bridport in 1938.

Thu Feb 9 to Sat Feb 11 1950
Showing of *The Third Man* – The Film You Have Been Waiting For. It had just won the Grand Prix at the Cannes Festival (Sep 17 1949), so the wait was not all that long. The firm returned to the Lyric in Oct 1954.

BN Mar 17 and 24 1950
The cinema advertisement asked: Have you entered the £1000 Bathing Beauty Competition? Full particulars on the Screen.

From the subsequent silence on the part of the BN one may assume that no local girl was the winner.

Tue Apr 18 to Sat Apr 22 1950
The BAODS production of "The Quaker Girl" – five evening performances and a Saturday matinee. From now until 1985 this will be the normal pattern.

Thu Jun 29 to Sat Jul 1 1950
Showing of Olivier's *Hamlet*, which in 1948 won Oscars for Best Picture, Best Actor, Best Art Direction and Best Costume Design. It was the first non-US film to receive the Academy Award for Best Picture.

Olivier's *Richard III* was given a week's run in 1956 (Jun 11–16).

Fri Jul 13 1951
The Chamber of Commerce Festival week (Jul 14–21) is inaugurated with the crowning of the Festival Queen, which "provided a pleasing interlude for those who attended the Palace Cinema, where the ceremony was performed by the Mayor, Coun. H. R. C. Palmer. Every seat was occupied and when, between the showing of the two

main films, the screen rose and revealed a gaily decorated stage in the midst of which stood a throne, the audience realised that it was a particularly fitting setting for such an auspicious occasion.

After the Mayor, supported by the President of the Chamber of Commerce, Mr A. D. Spencer, and other members had taken their places on the stage, the Queen-elect, Miss Joanna Harris, and her two attendants, Miss Hazel Roberts, of Eype, and Miss Jacqueline Weston, of Beaminster, made a triumphal entrance to the strains of martial music" (BN Jul 20 1951).

Seventeen-year-old Joanna Harris was the niece of the Rector of Bridport, Canon G. C. Clare, and was then resident at the Rectory. Her coronation ceremony began at about 8.45 p.m., just after the "B" picture *Blaze of Glory* (US 1950), a modest 66-min horse-racing tale, and before *Three Husbands* (US 1950), an attempt at sophisticated comedy. The titles are pleasingly appropriate.

Mon Sep 10 to Sat Sep 15 1951

"MEECH'S STUDIO, BRIDPORT presents on the stage every evening this week at 6.40 and 9.15 PROFESSOR RANGI, the amazing Hypnotist direct from New Zealand, soon to be presented in the largest halls throughout Great Britain."

A separate advertisement invited all to be hypnotised. "DO YOU want to Stop Smoking? Prof. Rangi can remove your Craving for Tobacco."

To experience this, you could choose between *The Laughing Lady*, a British musical with Anne Ziegler and Webster Booth (Mon–Wed) and *Belle Le Grand*, an incompetent American period melodrama (Thu–Sat).

Mon Sep 17 to Wed Sep 19 1951

Bridport is treated to the attractive sight of the voluptuous 19-year-old Silvana Mangano standing in the rice-fields of the Po Valley in *Bitter Rice*, the first major Continental film to be shown at the Palace since the war, but presumably in the dubbed version. (Sunday patrons had seen *Vengeance*, a minor and doubtless dubbed French thriller starring Viviane Romance back in Oct 1948.)

The programme for the second half of the week returned to the safer, inhibited British pleasures of *The Browning Version*.

The Lyric had shown Rossellini's *Stromboli* (with Ingrid Bergman) in April, in the truncated English version distributed by RKO.

Fri Jan 18 1952

On account of a special private viewing there is only one public evening showing of *Penny Points to Paradise*, 77 minutes of Harry Secombe, Peter Sellers, Alfred Marks and Spike Milligan, and *The Sleeping City*, an American hospital murder mystery.

Full details of this special event were given in the BN Jan 25 1952 in an article signed L.H.B.:

"THEY SAW THEMSELVES AS OTHERS SEE THEM
W. Dorset's staple trade makes good entertainment

Bridport networkers on Friday saw themselves as others will see them soon not only in the cinemas of Britain but on the screens of many overseas countries.

The occasion was the second performance at Bridport Palace Cinema last Friday when the house was reserved for employees of Bridport Industries Ltd, and a few guests, including the Mayor, Coun. H. R. C. Palmer, and Mayoress, Mrs A. J. Palmer, to see a private showing of the first talking picture made about the town and its trade.

The film, made by National Screen Services, with the cooperation of Bridport Industries Ltd, is one of a series entitled Come With Me and commentary and interviews are by Richard Dimbleby.

From braiders to directors the general opinion was that these glimpses of Bridport's ancient staple trade were not only entertaining, but should do a power of good in emphasising that this one-time seaside village craft is today a highly organised and very considerably mechanised industry.

An exceedingly satisfactory standard of photography was achieved by Norman Cobb, who was in charge of production, and after the showing of the film Mr Arnold Williams, Managing Director of National Screen Services, had a word with the audience to whom he was introduced on the stage by Mr H. N. Sanctuary, a Director of Bridport Industries. Mr Sanctuary was largely responsible for the technical detail of the picture.

The opening sequences are rich in scenic titbits. There were glimpses of many villages in the Bridport neighbourhood. Thatch, tower, spire and leafy lane were a perfect introduction to a series of outstanding pictures of the Dorset coast from Chesil Beach to Golden Cap.

This feast of panorama was completed at West Bay, where fishing and the sand and gravel trade were highlighted.

Redwing, manned by Mr Albion Whetham and Pilot Frank Butt, was seen fishing. Nets were hauled in and a truly magnificent lobster emerged from one of the pots. Also shown were Messrs Norman Good's team of horses hauling a load of gravel from the beach in the shadow of East Cliff – one of the picture prizes of the neighbourhood, as The Times once emphasised.

Mr Geoffrey Good was seen explaining to Mr Dimbleby the how and why of Bridport Harbour's sand exports, a sequence which included pictures of two Dutch motor vessels, berthed in the harbour.

Thence to the net industry, which had early been prefaced with King John's order for ropes for the Royal Navy of his day.

The processes of the net and line making were photographed at Messrs Hounsells in North Mills and at Messrs Edwards, Rendall and Coombs and Gales, Mr Frank Matterface was seen preparing hemp for the machines and all the processes of spinning were shown in detail. Machines net making, line walks, the making of tennis nets down to stitching in the bands, were all pictured.

It was natural that the sight of themselves on the screen gave many members of the audience much pleasure and not a little amusement.

One of the remarkable features of this Bridport film, the making of which began in August and which was finished just before Christmas, was the interior shots. These were all taken in a studio in London.

Here Mr Sanctuary was shown in his office explaining the net industry to Mr Dimbleby, Mr Dimbleby was seen chatting in a most realistic reproduction of the bar of the George Hotel, West Bay, with Mr Whetham and Mr Butt, and Mrs Olive Legg, of Loders, who won the braiding competition at the Bath and West Show last summer, was pictured in her cottage explaining to Mr Dimbleby the ways of her ancient craft.

Mr Geoff Good, too, appeared to be speaking to Mr Dimbleby with a background of heaped gravel and Pier Terrace in the middle distance, but this and all these practically perfect backgrounds were studio built.

The film is not faultless. A little more emphasis might have been given to not only the making of the nets and twines locally, but to the work they do and the dollars they earn.

Bridport's importance would undoubtedly have been enhanced in the eyes of the world if audiences had been shown a winning point at Wimbledon taken over a Bridport net, salmon being caught in Western Canada in Bridport nets, and herring and cod being landed in the North Sea drifters with Bridport nets and lines.

Apart from an excellent picture of South Street, taken near the Parish Church, Bridport appears to be a sleepy place and West Bay a forgotten backwater.

Of course a great deal more material was filmed than appears in this picture, and it is no easy matter to compress the life of Bridport and district into a 20-minute footage. On the other hand, a better job would have been done if a little less attention had been paid to scenery and a bit more to the town and its industry.

This said I think this Bridport Come With Me will make its mark. It will most certainly be an eye-opener to many who see it."

The article was headed by a photograph with the caption: "Richard Dimbleby interviews two locals – Messrs Albion Whetham and F. Butt. It looks very much like the bar at the George Hotel, West Bay, but this shot from the film of Bridport was taken in a London studio."

Mon Feb 25 to Sat Mar 1 1952
The special film of the funeral of George VI is shown at both the Palace and the Lyric for a week.

The King had died on Wed Feb 6 at the age of 56.

Mon Jul 28 to Wed Jul 30 1952
Showing of *A Streetcar Named Desire*, starring Vivien Leigh and Marlon Brando – the first X certificate film (adults only, unsuitable for those under 16) to reach Bridport. The Lyric revived it in Apr 1962.

Just under six months later in Jan 1953 *Detective Story* (US 1951) initiates at the Lyric what turns out to be a steady stream of X rated films.

By the time the Lyric closed more than 200 different X films had been shown in Bridport: 55 or so at the Palace, over 165 at the Lyric. Broadly speaking, these films were of three main types:

Quality dramas of a serious and genuinely adult nature, such as *Room at the Top, Look Back in Anger, Anatomy of a Murder, Peeping Tom, A Taste of Honey, La Dolce Vita, The Blackboard Jungle, The Man with the Golden Arm*. About 40% of the Palace's X films fall into this category, just over 15% of the Lyric's.

Horror, science fiction, monster and violent crime films, from *Psycho, Les Diaboliques/The Fiends* and the best Hammer films (*The Quatermass Experiment, The Curse of Frankenstein* etc.) to such epics as *The Blob, Attack of the Crab Monsters/50 Foot Woman, Godzilla, King of the Monsters* (from Japan), *I Was a Teenage Werewolf* and *The Killer Shrews*. More than half – nearly 60% – of the X films shown at the Lyric aimed to frighten and/or shock, while some 30% of the Palace's "adult" films were of this type.

Sex films, ranging from more or less witty comedies like *The Moon is Blue, The Little Hut, La Ronde*, via a sober account of natural childbirth (*The Case of Dr*

Laurent) and Maupassant stories (*Le Plaisir*, described as naughty but not scandalous) to titillation à la Bardot and exposés of prostitution, vice and assorted sleaze (*Call Girls, Women of Twilight* etc.). The Palace showed about 15 such films, including the neatly entitled *Bed Without Breakfast*. The Lyric's total was 40 or so, with one memorable programme in Sep 1955, consisting of *Unmarried Mothers*, "the story of a young girl caught in an odd web of circumstance. It is a clever Swedish drama", gamely supported by the British farce *Don't Blame the Stork* (only Cert A).

About 20% of the X films shown came from abroad, in particular France and Italy, but no indication was given as a rule in the BN advertisements as to the language on the soundtrack, and it is likely that some were dubbed. However, in 1957 the Lyric did reveal that three French films, *The Fiends, Mam'selle Striptease* (Cert A) and *The Light Across the Street* had English subtitles. No doubt the viewers of some of the sexier and sleazier movies were not much interested in dialogue and plot anyway.

BN Aug 22 1952

"Television came to Dorset last Friday with the official opening of the Wenvoe transmitter." Its effect on cinemagoing in Bridport would be profound.

Mon Jun 8 to Wed Jun 10 1953

Showing of a 3 Dimension film: the 13-min *A Day in the Country*, somewhat misleadingly advertised as "the latest sensation". It had been made in the US c. 1937 and was now reissued at a time when features in the new Natural Vision 3-D process – involving the wearing of grey polaroid spectacles by the audience, two synchronised projectors and a specially treated screen – were being released by Hollywood in an effort to entice people away from their television sets. This short, in which two boys get up to a series of pranks and then drive off in their father's car, was fairly primitive in style and technique and, having been shot in the earlier anaglyphic process, was viewed through coloured spectacles with one eyepiece red and the other green-blue.

Another 3-D short *Metroscopix* (Cert A), lasting 20 minutes and concluding with a Three Dimensional Murder sequence directed by George Sidney, was shown three-and-a-half weeks later, Jul 2–4 1953. Produced by MGM in 1935 and using the same anaglyphic process as *A Day in the Country* and Paramount's *Plastigrams* (see Jan 18–20 1926), the film "demonstrates the new 3-D as it shows a girl swinging out of the screen, right over the heads of the audience. Indian Clubs and thrown and seem to hurtle into the theatre, water from a fire hose appears to come from the screen – all these occur with startling reality, apparently putting each person in the audience in the middle of the action."

Stereoscopic films, of course, were not exactly new, and these two shorts did not in fact demonstrate the latest 3-D process, which had achieved great commercial success with the colour feature *Bwana Devil* (US 1952), a dire jungle film which Bridport was spared. One of the best of the very few Natural Vision movies was *House of Wax* (Cert X), starring Vincent Price and shown at the Palace Sep 27–29 1954. The BN advertisement described it as "the astounding and sensational mystery thriller in Warnercolor" and "strictly for adults only", but no mention was made of 3-D and the version projected was no doubt "flat".

The combination of special projection requirements, tiresome spectacles, frequent headaches, over-gimmicky second-rate films (with a lot of items being thrown at the audience) and the successful advent of Cinemascope brought about the rapid demise of 3-D colour features. This was a short-lived novelty, which in effect bypassed Bridport.

Mon Jun 22 to Sat Jun 27 1953

Showing of *A Queen is Crowned*, the full-length film of the Coronation in Glorious Technicolor. In this case "full-length" = 89 minutes.

"By the end of the week between 9,000 and 10,000 people will have seen the film 'A Queen is Crowned' at the Palace Cinema, Bridport. So great was the demand for seats for the show that four separate performances, instead of the usual two, were arranged for yesterday (Thursday), Friday and Saturday.

Coach loads of people from all parts of West Dorset have been amongst the patrons. On Monday a party of 70 old folk from Burton Bradstock were among the audience and on Tuesday the 'house' included another 60 old people in an organised party.

Members of the Shipton Gorge and Walditch W.I. have also taken advantage of this opportunity and other organised parties have come from Litton Cheney, Powerstock, Beaminster, Netherbury, Melplash, West Milton and Puncknowle.

Arrangements were also made for pupils from the Primary, Convent, St Mary's, Grammar, Allington, St Ronan's, General, Grove and Loders Schools, representing the 1,500 children of the Borough, to see the spectacular record of this great event.

The Headmaster of the Bridport Grammar School, Major Urwin Thornburn, told the *News* that Bridport teachers were so impressed by the film that they felt it was well worth sacrificing the equivalent of three equal periods of instruction in school in order to give the children an opportunity of a lesson on monarchy such as they were never likely to forget" (BN Jun 26 1953).

This initial run – with performances during the latter part of the week at 3.15, 5, 7.10 and 9 – coincided in part with the Bridport Royal Charter Pageant, the first performance of which took place on Wed Jun 24 from 2.45 to 5 p.m. in the presence of Princess Margaret.

The film was proudly re-presented at the Lyric for a further week (Jul 20–25) "in response to the request of numerous Patrons".

Elizabeth had been crowned in Westminster Abbey on Tue Jun 2 – the first coronation to be televised.

Mon Jan 25 to Wed Jan 27 1954

First showing of the highly successful British comedy *Genevieve*, rather surprisingly for three days only. However, it soon reappeared at the Lyric for three days in April (26–28), was back at the Palace in 1956 (Oct 8–10) with *Doctor in the House* in a "Stupendous Double Feature Programme in response to popular demand". That same programme turned up again at the Lyric for a week in early May 1960.

Mon Aug 16 to Sat Aug 21 1954

Doctor in the House, the first of the series of seven Doctor films made between 1954 and 1970, is shown for a week and is so popular that the BN Aug 27 comments on the phenomenon:

"More than 5,000 people saw the film Doctor in the House at the Palace Cinema, Bridport, last week. There were full houses for all the 13 performances and on some nights people had to be turned away. Every night long queues stretched down South Street and there were continuous lines of cars parked on both sides of the road."

It made its first return to the Palace for three days in mid-November (15–17).

Its successors all had an initial run at the Palace of a week: *Doctor at Sea*, which had the added attraction of Brigitte Bardot, in 1955 (Oct 3–8), *Doctor at Large* in 1957 (Jul 8–13), *Doctor in Love* in 1960 (Nov 28–Dec 3). *Doctor at Sea* turned up at the Lyric immediately before Christmas 1957.

Mon Mar 7 to Sat Mar 12 1955

Showing of *White Christmas*, the World First Motion Picture in VistaVision – startling CLARITY DETAIL REALISM SEEN WITHOUT EYE-STRAIN.

VistaVision was Paramount's widescreen process answer to 20th Century Fox's Cinemascope, both being developed to meet the challenge from television. VistaVision did not require the use of special anamorphic lenses and could be projected to suit screens of various sizes.

Mon Apr 23 to Sat Apr 28 1956

Cinemascope – the most successful of the widescreen processes – comes to Bridport with the showing of the British war film *Cockleshell Heroes*, in the week following the annual BAODS production. "After Saturday's finale of The Geisha, the Society's President, Mr H. R. C. Palmer, thanking the Dorchester Cinema Company for use of the Cinema, referred to the considerable extra expense the Board had gone to to ensure that their new cinemascope screen would be sufficiently mobile to enable the Society to stage future productions there" (BN Apr 27 1956).

New prices of admission were announced at this time: 3/3, 2/9, 2/3, 1/3 (including tax). Special prices for children under 14 years (except Sundays).

The story of *Cockleshell Heroes* had been serialised in the BN in five parts from Feb 3 to Mar 2 1956. No other film was to receive this special treatment.

The film was shown at the Lyric for three days in Apr 1957 and Jun 1958.

It is interesting to note that *The Robe*, the first film made in the Cinemascope process in 1953, did not reach the Palace until Dec 1959.

Tue Oct 23 to Wed Nov 7 1956

The period of the Hungarian National Rising (Oct 23–Nov 4) and the climax of the Suez Crisis (Oct 29–Nov 7).

During this critical fortnight the Palace offered its patrons three Westerns – the third (Nov 5–7) being *Tribute to a Bad Man – The Rains of Ranchipur*, featuring emotional and natural disaster in British India, and *Safari*, an Anglo-American amalgam of lion hunting and Mau Mau troubles. Meanwhile in Barrack Street on Oct 23 the Lyric was showing *The Day the World Ended*, and on Oct 29 *Illegal*.

BN Jun 7 1957

"Central figure in the Pathe film newsreel at the Palace and Lyric cinemas, Bridport, last Thursday, Friday and Saturday was Admiral Sir Dudley North, of Parnham Lodge, Beaminster.

The film, taken at Sir Dudley's home, discusses his fight to clear his name in the controversy regarding the escape of six French warships through the Straits of Gibraltar to Dakar in 1940.

Sir Dudley, who is 75, has been presented with a copy of the film by the Associated British Cinema's district supervisor, Mr Donald Shave."

Admiral Commanding the North Atlantic Station 1939–1940, he had been relieved of his command at Churchill's instigation. He lived at Netherbury House 1941–1955, died on May 15 1961 and was buried at sea several miles off Portland Bill three days later.

During the annual meeting of the West Dorset Conservative Association in Dorchester on Sat Jun 1, the constitutency MP, Mr Simon Wingfield Digby, discussed a number of local issues, including the decline in cinema audiences. "With the arrival of television, he said, the country cinemas were faced with growing difficulties. 'Maybe it is something which has to come – the cinemas in small country towns have to disappear for economic reasons – but I hope that they will not', he said. 'It would be a great pity, and I hope that anything possible which can be done by the Exchequer to ease their position will be done.'

The country cinemas, he said, provided entertainment in counties like Dorset, where distance was still a factor to be reckoned with."

The Bridport cinemas, of course, were not immune from these "growing difficulties".

BN Aug 23 1957

"A packed house at the Palace Cinema, Bridport, on Friday, saw the Mayor of Bridport, Coun. Miss M. G. Northover, present Mrs Margaret Sprackling, of 19 East Street, Bridport, with the £1000 cheque which she recently won in a National daily newspaper competition concerning do's and don'ts for safe motoring ... Afterwards the newspaper which organised the competition entertained Mrs Sprackling, her husband, the Mayor and other friends to a sherry party in the cinema."

BN Dec 13 1957

The cinemas feature in two linked items on the front page:

"'The dark shadow of unemployment hangs heavily over Bridport', Clr K. J. Clifford told Bridport Town Council on Tuesday. He said business in the shops had dropped, the cattle market had gone and he understood that one of the town's cinemas would shortly be closing."

"Questioned about remarks at the Town Council meeting concerning the closing of one of the town's cinemas, Mr S. C. Shepherd, Manager of both the Palace and Lyric Cinemas, told the 'News' that the rumour was unfounded.

'I have heard nothing at all about either of the cinemas closing', he said."

The Lyric was to survive for nearly five more years.

BN Jul 25 1958

During a meeting of the BAODS to decide on their next production, it is stated that the Palace Cinema has a total seating capacity of 2,922 for the six performances, i.e. it can seat 487 people at any one time.

Thu Jan 29 to Sat Jan 31 1959

Showing of *Carry on Sergeant*, the first of the highly successfully series of 30 comedies, each a traditionally English mixture of old farcical situations and well-worn comic postcard jokes and characters. The Palace showed it again in the spring of 1961.

The next five in the series all duly turned up at the Palace: *Carry on Nurse* (Aug 10–15 1959), *Carry on Teacher* (Apr 18–20 1960), *Carry on Constable* (Aug 8–13 1960), *Carry on Regardless* (Jul 10–15 1961), *Carry on Cruising* (Aug 16–18 1962). They were clearly ideal entertainment for the summer holiday crowds.

Each of these – except the last – reappeared later at the Lyric.

Another comic favourite of the period was Norman Wisdom, who had his first starring role in *Trouble in Store*, shown at the Palace May 31–Jun 2 1954, and then again at the Lyric in May 1956. His popularity meant that most of his subsequent films found their way to South and/or Barrack Street.

BN Feb 13 1959

"Tomorrow Mr S. C. Shepherd will go to Bridport's Palace Cinema for the last time as manager. He is retiring after 48 years connection with Bridport cinemas.

It was in 1911 that Mr Shepherd came to Bridport to open what is now the Lyric Cinema in Barrack Street and which was then called the Electric Palace. He formed a company in 1926 and it was then that the Palace Cinema in South Street was opened. In 1939 both the Palace and Lyric were taken over by the Dorchester Cinema Company.

Manager of the Lyric for 48 years and of the Palace for 33 years Mr Shepherd has been a familiar figure among picture goers in Bridport for almost half a century. He will be missed by local film enthusiasts.

During the First World War Mr Shepherd served in Belgium with the Hampshire Labour Corps and during his absence from Bridport, the Lyric was carried on by his sister, the late Mrs George Knight, and by Mr W. T. Ryan, who is succeeding Mr Shepherd as manager of the two cinemas. Indeed, Mr Ryan has been with Mr Shepherd as chief engineer for 46 years.

Born in Brixton, Mr Shepherd moved to Henley-on-Thames as a boy. Later he went to Reading and on to Littlehampton, Sussex, where his father opened a cinema. It was from Littlehampton that Mr Shepherd came to Bridport 48 years ago.

Interviewed in his office at the Palace by a 'News' reporter this week, Mr Shepherd recalled that in 1911 prices of admission at the Lyric were 3d, 6d and a shilling.

'Children were admitted for a penny to Saturday afternoon matinees and at Christmas they were each presented with an orange', he said.

Mr Shepherd, in his retirement, will continue to live at St Andrew's Road, Bridport.

He is married and has a son, Mr P. L. Shepherd, of Crawley, Sussex, who is in Rediffusion Ltd, and a daughter, Mrs W. T. Herring, of Cardiff, whose husband is an I.T.V. engineer. Mr Shepherd's son has just completed three years as a Radar Engineer in the R.A.F. as a Flying Officer.

Asked whether he would be going to the Palace after his retirement at all Mr Shepherd replied: 'I shall drop in to watch a good picture occasionally when one comes along'.

Then he added: 'I shall miss coming to the Palace tremendously; once you get into a trade, it gets under your skin'.

Mr Shepherd mentioned that talkies did not come to the Palace till 1931. 'In the five years from 1926 to 1931, when we had silent films, we had a pianist and a violinist to provide music', he said, as our reporter bade him farewell and left him sitting thoughtfully in his office for the last time – with a storehouse of memories."

When one recalls, for example, that the Electric Palace in Barrack Street opened in Feb 1912 and closed in May 1926 and that the Lyric did not open until Dec 1934, it is clear that a few minor details of the above report need to be amended. (See also BN Dec 22 1916.)

The programme at the Palace on Mr Shepherd's final Saturday evening was not all that inspiring, consisting of *No Time for Sergeants*, an American army comedy, and *Girl on the Subway*, originally made for TV and starring Natalie Wood.

The farewell party was reported in the BN Feb 29 1959: "The staffs of the Palace and Lyric Cinemas gathered in the lounge of the Palace on Tuesday afternoon to say farewell to Mr S. C. Shepherd, who retired the previous Saturday ...

Cashiers, usherettes, commissionaires, projectionists and cleaners saw Mr W. T. Ryan, who is succeeding Mr Shepherd as manager, present him with a fire screen cum coffee table to which they had all subscribed. Mr Ryan, who has been associated with Mr Shepherd in the business for 46 years, also handed him a box of cigarettes.

Mr Shepherd thanked the company most heartily for their gift. He expressed the wish that they would all support Mr Ryan as they had supported him. 'You all have a job to do', he added.

One of the staff wished Mr Shepherd a long and happy retirement. 'We have always been happy under you and I think Mr Ryan will also be all right towards us', she said.

'I shall try to keep you in order', remarked Mr Ryan amid laughter.

Mr Shepherd went on to say that he had had some happy times at the Palace and the Lyric. He recalled some of his experiences in the Cinemas and mentioned some amusing happenings of when the siren used to sound during the last War.

Mr J. Bartlett, chief projectionist, who has been at the Palace since 1934, told Mr Shepherd they had all been happy under his direction. They all hoped he had a long and happy retirement.

The happy party broke up everyone went back to their jobs and Mr Shepherd made his way home, proudly carrying the present that will for ever remind him of his 48 years as a cinema manager in Bridport.

On Saturday Mr Shepherd went to Dorchester where he received an electric clock and a cheque from the directors of the Dorchester Cinema Company, proprietors of both the Palace and Lyric Cinemas."

Mr and Mrs Shepherd left Bridport at the end of September 1962 to go and live with their married daughter. This was announced, with some biographical details, in the BN Sep 21 1962, and a fortnight later the newspaper contained the following report on page 13:

"A cheque for £21 10s was presented at St Andrew's Church Hall, Bridport, on Friday [i.e. Sep 28] to Mr and Mrs S. C. Shepherd, of Delapre-gardens, Bridport who are leaving the town to live with their daughter in Ipswich.

Making the presentation, the Rector of Bridport (the Rev. J. P. Hinton) spoke of the valuable services given to St Andrew's Church by both Mr and Mrs Shepherd.

Parishioners had contributed towards the cheque.

Mr Shepherd was treasurer of the church for 15 years and Mrs Shepherd was a Chapel Warden for ten.

The Mayor of Bridport (Clr Harold Smith), Chapel Warden at St Andrew's wished Mr and Mrs Shepherd every happiness in the future."

A photograph of the Rector presenting the cheque for Mr and Mrs Shepherd appeared on page 8 of this Oct 5 1962 issue.

Mr Shepherd died in 1968 in Scotland at the age of 84.

His direct involvement with Bridport's cinemas as manager spanned a period of 47 years, with just a brief break in the latter half of the Great War. His contribution to the general happiness and well-being of the inhabitants of Bridport and district from 1912 to 1959 was no doubt considerable and should perhaps be more widely recognised. It is remarkable that local histories have paid little or no attention to the important part played by the cinema in the social life of the town in this century.

Mon Jul 6 to Sat Jul 11 1959

Filming at West Bay and Eype of a large part of *The Navy Lark*, a b/w Cinemascope comedy based on a popular radio show and starring Ronald Shiner, Cecil Parker, Nicholas Phipps and Leslie Phillips.

On the Monday and Tuesday stars, director (Gordon Parry), producer (Herbert Wilcox), technicians etc. and H.M.S. Reedham, a minesweeper, arrived at West Bay, which was playing the part of an island port somewhere near the French coast housing a nearly forgotten and very corrupt minesweeping unit. Eype beach became the smugglers' cove. Shooting continued till the end of the week, with local extras employed for crowd scenes. On Sunday the whole company moved out, and pantechnicons loaded with equipment left for London to begin work at the Walton-on-Thames studios on Monday morning. (See BN Jul 10 and 17 1959.)

Mon Sep 14 to Wed Sep 16 1959

Showing of *Nudist Paradise* (Cert A), in Eastman Colour and Nudiscope, the first British nudist film, which concludes at Woburn Abbey and the Naturist World Congress.

A fairly brief period of on the whole innocuous naturist films (1957–61) opened in Bridport at the Lyric (Aug 11–13 1958) with *The Garden of Eden*, sponsored by the American Sunbathing Association, banned by the British censors in Jan 1955, but eventually granted an A certificate. The supporting film that August was *Female Jungle*, featuring the pneumatic Jayne Mansfield as a nymphomaniac. Three weeks later, Sep 1–3, Danish teenagers and others could be seen sunbathing on the celebrated *Isle of Levant*.

In 1959 the Lyric presented *Elysia (Land of the Sunworshippers)* at the beginning of March – a 1933 American film reissued in Aug 1958 to cash in on the current fashion – and in May *Adam and Eve* (Mexico, 1956), which could be described as the first religious nudist film.

The Palace kept to the home-grown product, following *Nudist Paradise* with *The Nudist Story* (Mon Feb 27 to Wed Mar 1 1961).

All these films had an A certificate.

Towards the end of this cycle of films the following item appeared in the BN Aug 25 1961:

"Films dealing with nudist camps are not new but it is still a little startling to find 'stills' of nudes outside cinemas. And perhaps it is a sign of the healthier attitude to the human body that photographs of nudes outside a Bridport cinema during the early part of this week have attracted so little comment.

Time was when there would have been indignant sermons from local pulpits and angry questions at the Town Council meeting. People living opposite the cinema tell us that a few elderly men have 'had their noses glued to the pictures' but although we pass the cinema two or three times a day, we have not noticed any adults or even teenagers who seemed particularly interested.

Two children under five were giving the pictures a second glance one morning but were a little reluctant to give the 'Bridport News' the benefit of their opinions. Eventually the little boy said he thought the pictures were 'rude' and his girl friend agreed with this point of view."

It is unfortunately impossible to identify cinema and film, as no Palace/Lyric advertisements appeared in the BN for nine weeks (Jul 28 to Sep 22 1962 inclusive). It is likely that the film was an X rated one – there were quite a few about at the time.

Mon Apr 11 1960

Supported by *Under Fire*, a minor American war film about deserters, *The Navy Lark* opens for a week's run just before Easter (no performance on Good Friday, of course), and Bridport flocks to see it, as the BN notes on Apr 22:

"CINEMA QUEUES!

These days business at the cinema is not as brisk as it was before television came on the scene. But last week it was 'just like the old days' at the Palace in Bridport.

The showing of The Navy Lark, Bridport's 'own film', brought large audiences to the cinema. There were even queues on most nights. The experience was a novel one for the newer members of the staff, who had never seen anything like it before.

But perhaps those who benefited most were the members of the Bridport Branch of the Royal Naval Association, who collected £37 from patrons leaving the cinema. The branch secretary (Mr W. R. N. Cast) said that the members were most grateful for the response to their appeal on behalf of naval charities."

The Navy Lark reappeared at the Palace for three days in 1962 (Nov 8–10).

Thu May 19 to Sat May 28 1960

An extended run of ten days – including Sunday – for The Greatest Picture of All Time, Cecil B. de Mille's *The Ten Commandments*, in VistaVision and Full Colour.

There is one performance only each evening at 6.40, as the film lasts nearly four hours (219 mins), and the admission prices are revised: Balcony 5/-, 3/6, Children 2/6. Stalls 3/6, 2/6, Children 2/6, 1/6. Complimentary list suspended.

De Mille's earlier 110-min silent version of *The Ten Commandments* (1923) had been shown at the Palace in Barrack Street for six days in Sep 1925.

Mon Jul 3 to Wed Jul 5 1961

Showing of Hitchcock's *Psycho*, with the warning: "It is essential to see this film from the beginning". It is also, of course, essential to have fairly strong nerves.

All 17 of Hitchcock's notable films of this period – from *Spellbound* (1945) and *Notorious* (1946) to *North by Northwest* (1959) and the murders at the Bates Motel – were shown in Bridport, eleven at the Palace, six at the Lyric (the less familiar ones). The Palace revived *Strangers on a Train* in 1962, ten years after its first run, and the Lyric re-presented *Notorious* in 1956, nine years after its first appearance at the Palace.

None of these films was given an unbroken six-day run.

Mon Mar 19 to Wed Mar 21 1962

Showing of Fellini's celebrated vision of contemporary spiritual and moral decay *La Dolce Vita*, certainly the most distinguished of the comparatively few foreign films exhibited at the Palace during this period (under 20, two-thirds of them X rated).

The Lyric was a little more adventurous in its programming. In addition to the 30 or so X films from abroad, it presented in the 1950s Rossellini's *Stromboli*, Silvana Mangano in *Anna* and *Ulysses*, *The Fall of Berlin* (a Soviet propaganda epic), Bunuel's splendid *The Adventures of Robinson Crusoe* (shot in Mexico), one or two Fernandel comedies, including the highly successful *The Sheep Has Five Legs*, the Swiss *Heidi and Peter* (a sequel to *Heidi*, shown at the Palace two years previously in 1954), Tati's classic *Monsieur Hulot's Holiday* (no language problems there!), Visconti's *The Wanton Countess/Senso*, René Clément's *The Sea Wall*, and in 1960 *The Wild Stallion/Crin Blanc* (a beautifully photographed study of a boy's relationship with a horse in the Camargue).

BN Jul 13 1962

It is reported that auditions for extras required for a scene of the film of *Tom Jones*, to be shot at Chilcombe during the next few weeks, are being held on Jul 12 and 13 at the Bridport Industries Social Club.

"The filming of this scene will take two or three days, but the actual date is not yet fixed and will be announced at the auditions. Those interested are asked to bring family, friends or relations who would also enjoy being in a film.

They can be any age, size, shape, they can be good-looking or otherwise. Just anyone and everyone, and the more the better. Even one-legged or one-armed people will be welcomed, specially 'casualties from the French wars' are wanted. Don't hesitate because the date might not suit you – come along and find out the actual dates you would be wanted and decide then."

Tom Jones (128 mins, Cert X) reached Bridport in late Oct 1963 and ran for a week, Oct 28–Nov 2, returning in 1964 for three days (Jun 1–3).

"Everyone in Bridport and a number of people from the surrounding district will be going to the Palace Cinema, South-street next week – some to see themselves and the rest to see their friends – on the screen!

The film 'Tom Jones' was screened (sic) in the West Dorset countryside and a number of Bridport people – interested in amateur dramatics – was engaged for several of the crowd scenes.

It had been suggested that the coming of the film to Bridport would provide the opportunity for a civic occasion and a 'get-together' for local people who took part in it, but the suggestion failed to materialise" (BN Oct 25 1963).

Sat Sep 1 1962

On this, the Lyric's last day, the Palace is showing *Road to Hong Kong*, made in a British studio on a small budget, the last and weakest of the seven Hope-Crosby-Lamour "Road" films.

All of them reached Bridport except, seemingly, the fourth: *Road to Utopia* (1945). They were often advertised incorrectly, acquiring an initial "The" – a fate suffered also by Disney's *Lady and the Tramp*, and by *House of Wax*.

Films shown in Bridport 1945–1962

Films given a week's run at the Palace

1948 *The Best Years of Our Lives* (Jun)
1951 *Alice in Wonderland* (Dec)
1952 *Captain Horatio Hornblower RN* (Jan)
1953 *The Cruel Sea* (Jun); *A Queen is Crowned* (Jun); *The Greatest Show on Earth* (Dec)
1954 *Doctor in the House* (Aug)
1955 *White Christmas* (Mar); *The Dam Busters* (Aug–Sep); *Doctor at Sea* (Oct)
1956 *Cockleshell Heroes* (Apr); *Richard III* (Jun); *A Town Like Alice* (Jul); *Reach for the Sky* (Aug); *The Man Who Never Was* (Sep); *The Baby and the Battleship* (Sep); *Trapeze* (Dec)
1957 *The Battle of the River Plate* (Mar); *High Society* (Apr); *Oklahoma* (May); *The King and I* (May–Jun); *Brothers in Law* (Jul); *Doctor at Large* (Jul); *Anastasia* (Jul–Aug); *The Admirable Crichton* (Sep); *Yangtse Incident* (Sep); *Island in the Sun* (Nov); *Heaven Knows, Mr Allison* (Dec)
1958 *The Bridge on the River Kwai* (May); *Blue Murder at St Trinian's* (Jun); *Happy Is the Bride* (Jun–Jul); *The Key* (Sep); *Dunkirk* (Sep); *The Wind Cannot Read* (Nov); *April Love* (Dec)
1959 *Room at the Top* (Jul); *Carry on Nurse* (Aug); *The Inn of the Sixth Happiness* (Nov–Dec)
1960 *I'm All Right, Jack* (Jan); *The Navy Lark* (Apr); *Northwest Frontier* (May); *The Ten Commandments* (May); *Expresso Bongo* (May–Jun); *Carry on Constable* (Aug); *Sink the Bismarck!* (Aug–Sep); *Around the World in Eighty Days* (Sep); *Doctor in Love* (Nov–Dec)
1961 *The Nun's Story* (Feb); *Saturday Night and Sunday Morning* (May); *Carry on Regardless* (Jul); *Swiss Family Robinson* (Dec)
1962 *One Hundred and One Dalmations* (Mar); *Gigi* (Mar); *The Young Ones* (Apr); *The Parent Trap* (Apr); *Only Two Can Play* (Jun); *Blue Hawaii* (Jun); *The Guns of Navarone* (Jul); *South Pacific* (Aug)

Films given a week's run at the Lyric

1949 *Forever Amber* (Jan)
1951 *On the Riviera* (Dec)
1952 *The Greatest Show on Earth* (Aug)
1953 *The World in His Arms* (Mar); *A Queen is Crowned* (Jul); *Pony Express* (Dec)
1956 *Reach for the Sky* (Nov); *Davy Crockett* (Dec)
1957 *Rock Around the Clock* (Jan); *Don't Knock the Rock* (Apr); *The Tommy Steele Story* (Jul); *Gone with the Wind* (Oct)
1958 *The Pride and the Passion* (Apr); *6.5 Special* (May); *Three Ring Circus* (Dec)
1959 *Girls at Sea* (Apr); *Lady and the Tramp* (Dec)
1960 *The Night We Dropped a Clanger* (Apr); *Doctor in the House/Genevieve* (May); *The Rough and the Smooth* (May); *Serious Charge* (Jun–Jul – Cliff Richard's debut)
1961 *The Greatest Show on Earth* (Dec – third time in Bridport)

Major British films shown for three days at the Palace

1945 *The Thief of Bagdad*
1946 *Perfect Strangers*; *The Halfway House*; *Love on the Dole*
1947 *Piccadilly Incident*; *The Courtneys of Curzon Street*
1948 *Mine Own Executioner*; *An Ideal Husband*; *Millions Like Us*; *Brief Encounter*; *Spring in Park Lane*; *Great Expectations*; *Blithe Spirit*; *Anna Karenina*; *Green for Danger*; *Mr Perrin and Mr Traill*
1949 *The Red Shoes*; *The Winslow Boy*; *Quartet*; *The Fallen Idol*; *Scott of the Antarctic*; *Maytime in Mayfair*; *The Small Back Room*; *The Glass Mountain*
1950 *The Third Man*; *The Blue Lamp*; *Hamlet*; *Passport to Pimlico*; *The Happiest Days of Your Life*; *The Chiltern Hundreds*; *The Wooden Horse*
1951 *Odette*; *Seven Days to Noon*; *Pandora and the Flying Dutchman*; *The Clouded Yellow*; *The Browning Version*; *White Corridors*
1952 *The Lavender Hill Mob*; *The Tales of Hoffmann*; *Laughter in Paradise*; *The Lady with a Lamp*; *Encore*; *Where No Vultures Fly*; *The African Queen*; *Outcast of the Islands*; *Love Story* ("introducing the famous Musical Composition 'Cornish Rhapsody'"); *Angels One Five*; *The Card*; *Mandy*
1953 *The Gift Horse*; *The Importance of Being Earnest*; *The Sound Barrier*; *Cry the Beloved Country*; *Ivanhoe*; *The Pickwick Papers*; *The Crimson Pirate*; *The Final Test*; *The Titfield Thunderbolt*; *The Captain's Paradise*
1954 *Malta Story*; *Genevieve*; *Moulin Rouge*; *Albert RN*; *The Kidnappers*; *Hobson's Choice*; *Knave of Hearts* (first British feature film to be X rated); *An Inspector Calls*
1955 *Father Brown*; *The Purple Plain*; *Romeo and Juliet*; *Carrington V.C.*; *The Colditz Story*; *The Prisoner*
1956 *Joe Macbeth*; *The Ladykillers*
1957 *Moby Dick*; *The Smallest Show on Earth*
1958 *The Prince and the Showgirl*; *Woman in a Dressing Gown*; *Lucky Jim*; *Carve Her Name with Pride*; *Orders to Kill*; *A Tale of Two Cities*; *Dracula*
1959 *A Night to Remember*; *Ice Cold in Alex*; *I Was Monty's Double*; *Tiger Bay*; *Danger Within*; *The Horse's Mouth*

1960   *Look Back in Anger; Sapphire; Our Man in Havana; The Battle of the Sexes; Two Way Stretch; The Angry Silence; The League of Gentlemen*

1961   *Peeping Tom; The Entertainer; Brides of Dracula; Saturday Night and Sunday Morning; Tunes of Glory; The Criminal; No Love for Johnnie; A Town Like Alice*

1962   *Whistle Down the Wind; A Taste of Honey*

Major British films shown for three days at the Lyric

1947   *Oliver Twist*

1949   *Saraband for Dead Lovers; Holiday Camp; The Seventh Veil; Miranda; London Town* (featuring the comedian Sid Field); *Hue and Cry; Caesar and Cleopatra; The Way to the Stars; It Always Rains on Sunday; The History of Mr Polly; Whisky Galore; The Rake's Progress*

1950   *Pink String and Sealing Wax; Kind Hearts and Coronets; The Captive Heart; The Wicked Lady*

1951   *I See a Dark Stranger; The Guinea Pig; The Overlanders; Dead of Night; The Hasty Heart; They Were Not Divided; Morning Departure; So Long at the Fair; Dance Hall; Trio*

1952   *No Highway; Brighton Rock; The Man in the White Suit; The Magic Box; Secret People*

1954   *The Maggie*

1958   *Barnacle Bill*

1960   *The Mouse That Roared; S.O.S. Pacific* (partly shot at Weymouth); *Libel*

1961   *Conspiracy of Hearts*

1962   *The Sundowners; Greyfriars Bobby*

As the above lists indicate, this was a period in which the British studios turned out a considerable number of good and entertaining films.

Major American films shown for three days at the Palace

1945   *Arsenic and Old Lace; Sunday Dinner for a Soldier; To Have and Have Not; Meet Me in St Louis*

1946   *Lady Hamilton; National Velvet; The Mask of Dimitrios; Mr Skeffington; Kitty; Anchors Aweigh; Rhapsody in Blue; Confidential Agent; The Lost Weekend; Ziegfeld Follies; The Blue Dahlia; The Postman Always Rings Twice; Cover Girl*

1947   *Mildred Pierce; The Spiral Staircase; The Bells of St Mary's; Rebecca; Gilda; The Southerner; The Jolson Story; A Night in Casablanca; Spellbound; The Diary of a Chambermaid; Notorious; Lady in the Lake; The Big Sleep*

1948   *Humoresque; The Yearling; Duel in the Sun; To the Ends of the Earth; The Woman on the Beach; Fort Apache*

1949   *Red River; I Remember Mama; Sorry, Wrong Number; The Paleface; The Secret Life of Walter Mitty; The Treasure of the Sierra Madre*

1950   *The Set Up; Johnny Belinda; The Red Pony; Home of the Brave; She Wore a Yellow Ribbon*

1951   *Panic in the Streets; All About Eve; The Men; Born Yesterday*

1952 *Strangers on a Train; Cyrano de Bergerac; A Streetcar Named Desire; Leave Her to Heaven; High Noon; Rommel, Desert Fox; Rancho Notorious; Five Fingers; The Quiet Man*
1953 *Annie Get Your Gun; Road to Bali; Limelight; Niagara*
1954 *Hans Christian Andersen; Roman Holiday; Call Me Madam; Quo Vadis; The Band Wagon; Shane; From Here to Eternity; Mogambo; The Big Heat; The Glenn Miller Story; Androcles and the Lion; House of Wax; It Should Happen to You; Calamity Jane; Johnny Guitar; Knock on Wood*
1955 *Dial M for Murder; The Caine Mutiny; Magnificent Obsession; On the Waterfront; Sabrina Fair; Rear Window; Bad Day at Black Rock; The Barefoot Contessa; Seven Brides for Seven Brothers; Marty*
1956 *The Man from Laramie; To Catch a Thief; Picnic; A Star Is Born; Mister Roberts; Lady and the Tramp; The Court Jester*
1957 *The Man Who Knew Too Much; Forbidden Planet; The Searchers; Friendly Persuasion; Funny Face; Guys and Dolls*
1958 *War and Peace; Giant; 3.10 to Yuma; Sweet Smell of Success; Gunfight at the O.K. Corral; Paths of Glory; Pal Joey; Witness for the Prosecution; Les Girls; Sayonara*
1959 *Vertigo; The Defiant Ones; The Young Lions; The Vikings; Cat on a Hot Tin Roof; Separate Tables; The Big Country*
1960 *Rio Bravo; Some Like It Hot; I Want to Live; Operation Petticoat; The Horse Soldiers; North by Northwest; On the Beach; Anatomy of a Murder*
1961 *The Apartment; Psycho; The Misfits* (the last film of Clark Gable and Marilyn Monroe, script by Arthur Miller)
1962 *The Magnificent Seven; Breakfast at Tiffany's; One-Eyed Jacks*

Major American films shown for three days at the Lyric

1946 *The Miracle of Morgan's Creek; Five Graves to Cairo; Ministry of Fear; The Uninvited*
1949 *The Naked City; Call Northside 777; The Bishop's Wife; Monsieur Verdoux; Road to Rio; A Foreign Affair; The Paradine Case; Rope; Yellow Sky*
1950 *Easter Parade; State Fair; Letter from an Unknown Woman; Pinky; Twelve O'Clock High; White Heat; The Snake Pit*
1951 *All the King's Men; The Gunfighter; Fourteen Hours; Winchester 73; Union Station; Sunset Boulevard*
1952 *Samson and Delilah; The Day the Earth Stood Still; A Place in the Sun; Viva Zapata; Carrie; Mourning Becomes Electra*
1953 *Singin' in the Rain; An American in Paris; Detective Story; Monkey Business; Gone with the Wind; Stalag 17; Come Back, Little Sheba; Murder, Inc.*
1954 *My Cousin Rachel; I Confess; Young Bess; Lili*
1955 *Executive Suite; Champion; the Bridges at Toko-Ri; Riot in Cell Block 11; Them!; Down Three Dark Streets; Gentlemen Prefer Blondes*
1956 *Man without a Star; The Blackboard Jungle; The Man with the Golden Arm; The Trouble with Harry*
1957 *I'll Cry Tomorrow; The Bad Seed* ("The National Press raved about this picture"); *Autumn Leaves; Twelve Angry Men; Baby Doll; East of Eden*
1958 *The Wrong Man; End as a Man; Time Limit*
1959 *The Old Man and the Sea*

1961   *Inherit the Wind; Elmer Gantry*
1962   *Too Late Blues; Paris Blues; The Absent-Minded Professor*

The films of Abbott and Costello and those featuring Betty Grable continued to be very popular after the war, while Elvis Presley became visible and audible on the big screen from the late 1950s. Younger Bridport audiences were exposed in the early 1950s to the series of low-budget *Bomba (the Jungle Boy)* films; these sub-Tarzan epics were not for the discerning.

As usual both cinemas presented a number of interesting non-fiction, documentary films, e.g. at the Palace:

The Conquest of Everest (3/54), the Disney True Life Adventure features *The Vanishing Prairie* (10/55) and *The Living Desert* (10–11/55), Lindsay Anderson's lyrical *Every Day Except Christmas* (2/59), a celebration of ordinary working people in Covent Garden Market, and Karel Reisz's *We Are the Lambeth Boys* (3/61), a study of the members of a London Youth Club;

and at the Lyric:

XIVth Olympiad: The Glory of Sport (1/49), Humphrey Jennings' *The Cumberland Story* (12/49) about the modernisation of the mining industry, *Three Dawns to Sydney* (3/50), made for BOAC to promote air travel, and *School for Danger* (8/50), originally entitled *Now It Can Be Told*, a reenactment by Capt. Harry Rée – later Headmaster of Watford Grammar School and Professor of Education at York University – of his work organising local resistance activities in France in 1943.

Revivals and re-issues

Some films first shown in Bridport BEFORE *the 1939–45 War which reappeared during this period as main features for a three-day run (with year of initial showing)*

At the Palace

1946   *The Barretts of Wimpole Street* (35); *Stella Dallas* (39); *Lloyds of London* (37); *Wings of the Morning* (37); *Stagecoach* (39); *A Yank at Oxford* (39); *The Sign of the Cross* (36); *Lives of a Bengal Lancer* (35); *The Private Life of Henry VIII* (34)
1947   *The Scarlet Pimpernel* (36); *The Thirty-Nine Steps* (36)
1948   *Bonnie Scotland* (36); *Sanders of the River* (35); *Elephant Boy* (37); *The Drum* (39); *Little Lord Fauntleroy* (37)
1949   *Under Two Flags* (36); *Nothing Sacred* (39); *Hurricane* (39)
1950   *Stagecoach* (39 – again)
1951   *Victoria the Great* (38); *Lost Horizon* (38); *The Prisoner of Zenda* (38)
1953   *Captain Blood* (36)
1954   *Lives of a Bengal Lancer* (35 – again)
1955   *Snow White and the Seven Dwarfs* (38); *Modern Times* (36)

At the Lyric

1945 *Dodsworth* (37); *A Star Is Born* (38); *Topper* (38); *It's in the Air* (39); *Queen of Hearts* (36); *Lorna Doone* (35)

1946 *Koenigsmark* (36); *The Firefly* (38); *David Copperfield* (35 – "specially selected cast of 65 stars"); *Maytime* (38); *Kid Millions* (35); *Night Must Fall* (38); *A Night at the Opera* (37); *The Adventures of Marco Polo* (39); *The Kid from Spain* (34)

1947 *Abraham Lincoln* (31); *The Ware Case* (39)

1951 *Top Hat* (36)

1953 *Desire* (37)

1955 *The Plainsman* (37)

1956 *Tarzan the Ape Man* (32)

1958 *San Francisco* (37)

1960 *All Quiet on the Western Front* (31 – "The Greatest Picture of All Time"); *The Plainsman* (37 – again)

In May 1949 Flaherty's *Nanook of the North* returned as an exceptional second feature. It had first been shown at the Palace in Barrack Street in Mar 1923. This was a 50-min sound-film version, released in July 1947.

In early Jan 1957 *The Gold Rush* was shown in a revised version with words and music added, which Chaplin had re-released for the second time in Apr 1956.

Some films first shown in Bridport DURING *the 1939–45 War which reappeared during this period as main features for a three-day run (with year of initial showing*

At the Palace

1946 *This Is the Army* (44); *Hatter's Castle* (43); *Tin Pan Alley* (41); *The Wizard of Oz* (40); *Bitter Sweet* (41)

1947 *I Met a Murderer* (39)

1948 *The Four Feathers* (40); *They Died with Their Boots On* (43); *South American George* (42); *The Ghost of St Michael's* (41); *Much Too Shy* (43)

1949 *Western Approaches* (45); *Wuthering Heights* (40); *Major Barbara* (42); *Ladies in Retirement* (42)

1950 *Holiday Inn* (43)

1954 *The Cat and the Canary* (40)

1955 *Goodbye Mr Chips* (40)

1956 *The Wizard of Oz* (40 – again)

At the Lyric

1945 *Across the Pacific* (43); *They Died with Their Boots On* (43)

1946 *Let George Do It* (41); *Thunder Rock* (43); *Strike Up the Band* (41)

1947 *Queen Victoria* (43); *The Night Has Eyes* (42); *Get Cracking* (43); *Bell Bottom George* (44); *Tomorrow We Live* (43); *The Real Glory* (40)

1949   *The Little Foxes* (41); *For Whom the Bell Tolls* (45); *Night Train to Munich*
       (41); *In Which We Serve* (43); *Only Angels Have Wings* (40)
1950   *Wuthering Heights* (40); *Going My Way* (45)
1952   *In Which We Serve* (43 – again)
1953   *Road to Zanzibar* (42); *My Friend Flicka* (45)
1954   *Beau Geste* (40); *Road to Singapore* (40); *Pride and Prejudice* (41); *Double
       Indemnity* (45)
1955   *Lassie Come Home* (44); *For Whom the Bell Tolls* (45 – again)
1956   *Thousands Cheer* (44); *Road to Morocco* (43)
1957   *The Sea Hawk* (41)
1958   *Random Harvest* (44)
1959   *Northwest Mounted Police* (42); *Gulliver's Travels* (40)
1960   *Wuthering Heights* (40 – again)

Some films first shown in Bridport AFTER *the 1939–45 War which were
given a second – and sometimes a third – run of at least three days as
main feature*

At the Palace

1948   *The Courtneys of Curzon Street; The Halfway House; The Thief of Bagdad;
       Spring in Park Lane*
1950   *Maytime in Mayfair; The Blue Lamp*
1951   *Cover Girl; The Red Pony*
1953   *The Greatest Show on Earth*
1954   *Limelight; Duel in the Sun; Doctor in the House*
1955   *The Blue Dahlia; The Quiet Man; High Noon; The Paleface*
1956   *The Kidnappers; The Glenn Miller Story; Genevieve; Doctor in the House*
1957   *Calamity Jane*
1958   *Lady and the Tramp; Annie Get Your Gun*
1960   *The King and I; The Secret Life of Walter Mitty*
1961   *Shane; Carousel*
1962   *East of Eden; Oklahoma*

[The interval between first and second runs varies from eight-and-a-half weeks to
eleven years.]

At the Lyric

1949   *The Red Shoes*
1950   *The Best Years of Our Lives*
1951   *Arsenic and Old Lace*
1953   *The Thief of Bagdad*
1954   *The Hasty Heart; Genevieve; The Jolson Story; The Third Man*
1955   *Captain Horatio Hornblower RN; No Highway*
1956   *The Spiral Staircase; The Dam Busters; Two Years Before the Mast; The
       Belles of St Trinian's; The Quatermass Experiment; The African Queen;*

Trouble in Store; From Here to Eternity; The Cruel Sea; Union Station; Road to Rio; Reach for the Sky; The Gift Horse

1957 *Cockleshell Heroes; Gone with the Wind; Doctor at Sea*

1958 *Shane; The Baby and the Battleship; The Yangtse Incident; Cockleshell Heroes; From Here to Eternity; Knock on Wood; The Big Heat; High Society; Anchors Aweigh; The Court Jester; The Tommy Steele Story*

1959 *White Christmas; Witness for the Prosecution; The Barefoot Contessa; The Blackboard Jungle; The Moon Is Blue; Dunkirk; Friendly Persuasion; I'll Cry Tomorrow; The Crimson Pirate; Carve Her Name with Pride; Phantom of the Rue Morgue; Ice Cold in Alex; Lady and the Tramp*

1960 *Lucky Jim; Room at the Top; The Paleface; Ivanhoe; Doctor in the House; Genevieve; Mogambo; The War of the Worlds; Up in Arms; The Quiet Man; The Searchers; Rio Bravo; The Purple Plain; Two Way Stretch*

1961 *Some Like It Hot; High Society; Calamity Jane; Hans Christian Andersen; The Best Years of Our Lives; The World in His Arms; The Seven Deadly Sins; The Curse of Frankenstein; Darby O'Gill and the Little People; Never on Sunday; The League of Gentlemen; Circus of Horrors; Horrors of the Black Museum; The Nun's Story; Macabre; The Dam Busters; The Greatest Show on Earth*

1962 *I Was Monty's Double; Gunfight at the O.K. Corral; Singin' in the Rain; the Gunfighter; A Streetcar Named Desire; House of Wax; Phantom of the Rue Morgue; Reach for the Sky; Duel in the Sun; Malta Story; Room at the Top; They Were Not Divided; The Cruel Sea; Dracula; The Mummy; The War of the Worlds; On the Waterfront; One Hundred and One Dalmations*

[The interval between first and second runs varies from 13 weeks to well over 13 years.]

As the above lists demonstrate, both Bridport cinemas revived or re-presented popular films during this period, some more than once and some from a comparatively distant past, with the Lyric's weekday programmes including roughly twice as many re-runs as the Palace's. The Sunday films at the Palace were nearly all revivals too, of course.

If a film is really worth seeing, it can bear repeated viewing, and most of the films that were given more than one run are arguably in that select category.

Postscript

1962–1997 A few landmarks

1962

Mon Nov 26–Sat Dec 1: Showing of the three-and-a-half hour Technicolor remake of *Ben Hur*. "Apart from its obvious appeal to churchmen, the film has something for everyone and brings the gospel story to the screen with vivid realism" (see Jan 9–14 1928).

1963

Thu Apr 18–Sat Apr 20: First showing of *Dr No*, the first Bond film.
Mon Sep 2: Death of William Thomas Ryan at the age of 67. He had succeeded Sydney Shepherd as manager of the Palace and Lyric (1959–61), having worked with him as operator/projectionist/chief engineer for 46 years.
Mon Oct 28–Sat Nov 2: First showing of *Tom Jones* – "Bridport Folk on the Screen".

1966

Sun Jun 5–Wed Jun 8: Showing of Russ Meyer's *Fanny Hill: Memoirs of a Woman of Pleasure* (US/W. Ger, 1964), "the film to which the British Board of Film Censors refused to give a certificate, but which Dorset County Council's General Purposes Committee is allowing to be shown in Dorset". An updated version of these notorious memoirs, *The Swedish Fanny Hill* (Cert X), ran for a week Nov 10–15 1969, supported by a feature-length Swiss survey of the *Pleasures of the Bath* (Cert A).

1968

Wed Jan 24–Sat Jan 27: Bridport Pantomime Players' first production at the Palace – Red Riding Hood.
Mon Jul 1–Sat Jul 6: First showing of *Far From the Madding Crowd* – over 50 people from the Bridport area took part as extras.

1969

Jan: Myles Byrne, owner of cinemas in the South (headquarters: Brighton), takes over the Dorchester Cinema Company and thereby the running of the Bridport Palace and the Dorchester Plaza. Both cinemas are to be modernised and redecorated.

1983

Fri Jan 7: The Bridport News draws attention to the threat to the cinema industry posed by video, Channel 4 and the possibility of cable television. "It is up to all those who still believe in the magic of the movies to ensure they survive into the 21st century."

1984

Thu Dec 6: On and from this date the Palace is closed on Thursdays as an economy measure.

1985

Fri Feb 15: A letter in the Bridport News recounts the experience of going to see *Gremlins* at the Palace on Sat Feb 9 and having the evening ruined by the behaviour of youngsters in the audience.

Mar: Rundown appearance of cinema and lack of publicity stills arouse fears of imminent closure, denied by Myles Byrne.

1986

Aug: Following the death of Myles Byrne, the Palace comes under new management, i.e. Stephen Wischusen and Maelor Jones, based at the Dome cinema, Worthing. Seven-day opening is restored from Fri Aug 29.

1992

Feb: Lease of the Palace is taken over by Barry Kavanagh and Mike Vickers. Known as Reeltime Entertainment, the organisation also runs the Plaza, Dorchester, the Torbay Picture House, Paignton, the Carlton, Westgate-on-Sea and the Kavanagh, Herne Bay.

1996

Fri Jun 14: The Mayor (Mrs Joyce Dunford) unveils the Cinema 100 plaque in the Palace foyer on the cinema's 70th birthday.

Mon Nov 18: Bridport Film Society celebrates 100 Years of Cinema, 84 years of filmgoing in Bridport, 70 years of the Palace and 47 years of Sydney Shepherd's management with a showing of *The Third Man*. Sydney Shepherd's son and daughter are present.

1997

Wed Nov 5: World première of *The Scarlet Tunic*, an adaptation of Thomas Hardy's short story "The Melancholy Hussar of the German Legion", filmed around Seatown, Chideock and Bridport in the autumn of 1996. Organised by the Palace manager, Graham Frampton, and sponsored by the Bridport News, the town council and local firms (with profits going to the Diana, Princess of Wales Memorial Fund), the gala evening began with a half-hour concert by the St Swithun's Silver Band and was attended by the Mayor, Councillor Bryan Rowe, the film's director, Stuart St Paul, and several members of the cast, including Emma Fielding and Gareth Hale.